This book will be a tremendous guide to the servants of God. Rooted firmly in biblical teaching and with practical application, David Cannistraci leads the Church to an understanding of true apostleship.

DR. PAUL K. ARIGA, PRESIDENT
All Japan Revival Mission, Kobe, Japan

Are apostles alive and well today? As we approach the twenty-first century, the apostles are being revealed as the last gift restored to the church. **Apostles and the Emerging Apostolic Movement** gives a clear definition of apostles and their restoration to the Body of Christ. Dr. David Cannistraci has done a thorough job of researching a little-understood truth. I highly recommend this book.

APOSTLE EMANUELE CANNISTRACI, PASTOR
Evangel Christian Fellowship

I thank God for Pastor David Cannistraci for tackling the subject of the apostle. He clearly, definitively and fairly brings us to a place of understanding this wonderful office that is so necessary to the Body of Christ.

ED DELPH, PASTOR
Hosanna Christian Fellowship

Thank God for this book! This vital and important information is needed by the Church to fulfill its destiny of reaching the world with the goodness of Jesus Christ!

JOHN ECKHARDT, PASTOR
Crusaders Ministries

I believe David Cannistraci's book, **Apostles and the Emerging Apostolic Movement** will be the first of many works to usher in apostolic fathering ministries. This book will clear up misconceptions while laying a firm foundation for true apostolic ministries.

DR. GARY L. GREENWALD, PASTOR
Eagle's Nest Ministries

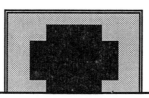

APOSTLES AND THE EMERGING APOSTOLIC MOVEMENT

DAVID CANNISTRACI

Renew

A Division of Gospel Light
Ventura, California, U.S.A.

Published by Renew Books
A Division of Gospel Light
Ventura, California, U.S.A.
Printed in U.S.A.

Renew Books is a ministry of Gospel Light, an evangelical Christian publisher dedicated to serving the local church. We believe God's vision for Gospel Light is to provide church leaders with biblical, user-friendly materials that will help them evangelize, disciple and minister to children, youth and families.

It is our prayer that this Renew book will help you discover biblical truth for your own life and help you meet the needs of others. May God richly bless you.

For a free catalog of resources from Renew Books and Gospel Light please call your Christian supplier, or contact us at 1-800-4-GOSPEL *or at* www.gospellight.com.

Previously published as *The Gift of Apostle.*

Library of Congress Cataloging-in-Publication Data
    Apostles and the Emerging Apostolic Movement / David Cannistraci
    ISBN 0-8307-2338-2 (trade paper)
    99-181990

2   3   4   5   6   7   8   9   10   11   12   13   14   15   16   /   03   02   01   00   99

Rights for publishing this book in other languages are contracted by Gospel Literature International (GLINT). GLINT also provides technical help for the adaptation, translation and publishing of Bible study resources and books in scores of languages worldwide. For further information, write to GLINT at P.O. Box 4060, Ontario, CA 91761-1003, U.S.A. You may also send e-mail to Glintint@aol.com, or visit their web site at www.glint.org.

To all those who follow the apostolic call:

The pioneers who have paid
the price to make a way,
The young apostles who stand
ready to be raised up,
And the generation that will arise
to claim the harvest.

CONTENTS

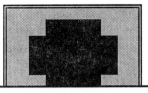

FOREWORD

DURING THE YEARS I HAVE BEEN A CHRISTIAN, I HAVE FREQUENTLY HEARD leaders consider the first-century church a model against which we should compare our contemporary church life. The idea is that the further we find ourselves from the Early Church, led by the apostles, the weaker we will probably be. Therefore, in our teaching, in our planning and in our daily activities we should strive to become more like the church of the first century.

Through more than four decades of Christian service, my primary sphere of activity and identity has been in the traditional evangelical camp. Fuller Theological Seminary, where I studied and teach, was originally founded to provide the mainline denominations in the United States a place where their leaders could receive a more conservative and biblically based theological foundation than many of their own seminaries were offering. Our primary church model was the church of the apostolic age.

Curiously, until fairly recently, I did not notice what now appears to me to be an inherent inconsistency in what I had been taught: *Our ideal was the Church led by the apostles, but supposedly no such apostles were to be found in our churches today!* Having accepted such a premise, it would then become clear that we could replicate the first-century church today only if the apostles were a trivial or relatively insignificant component of first-century Christianity. No biblical scholar I know, however, would affirm that. Apostles were a recognized *key* to the vitality of the Early Church.

When I wrote my book *Your Spiritual Gifts Can Help Your Church*

Grow (Regal Books) years ago, I found myself arguing that no com-pelling biblical evidence appears to indicate that certain spiritual gifts, including the gift of apostle, had ceased at the close of the apostolic age, as some of my seminary professors had taught, and as I had believed for some time. I became more convinced of this than ever when more recently I completed my three-volume commentary of the book of Acts (Regal Books). I now believe we can begin to approach the spiritual vitality and power of the first-century church *only* if we recognize, accept, receive and minister in all the spiritual gifts, including the gift of apostle.

Is such a thing possible? I believe it is. My studies of church growth have led me to an inexorable conclusion: The fastest-growing identifi-able segment of Christianity in the 1990s on five continents is what has come to be called the Postdenominational Movement. Inherent in today's postdenominational churches is a structure commonly known as "apostolic networks," in which both the gift and office of apostle are recognized and accepted.

Having arrived at that point in my own thinking and spiritual development, I was ready for that remarkable day when the United States mail brought to me David Cannistraci's manuscript *Apostles and the Emerging Apostolic Movement.* I devoured it in one reading, after which I praised God in an increasing crescendo for providing a tool for those of us who are serious about going back to first-century Christianity, which is desperately needed. We now have a well-researched, field-tested, mature and biblically balanced textbook about the gift of apostle and how it can function in churches today.

David Cannistraci, a key figure in the Postdenominational Movement, is a person of giftedness, wisdom and experience beyond his years. He is one of those rare people who is seen simultaneously as a scholar and a practitioner. Not only does Dr. Cannistraci develop the-ories, but he also makes sure his theories have gone through hands-on experimentation before he advocates them. I will require my Fuller Seminary students to read and digest this book.

The days in which we live are not normal times. We have moved into a season of the greatest outpouring of the power of the Holy Spirit and the greatest harvest of souls in all of Christian history. Business as usual will not suffice in our churches and ministries today! David Cannistraci's is one of the clear voices that will help the Body of Christ meet the crucial spiritual challenges that face us. You will understand what I mean as you read this book.

C. Peter Wagner
Fuller Theological Seminary
Pasadena, California

ACKNOWLEDGMENTS

MANY WONDERFUL PEOPLE HAVE "SUPPORTED MY HANDS" (SEE EXOD. 17:12) during the process of writing this book. There is no way to express how marvelous my support network is! No meaningful accomplishment is ever the result of one person, and I gratefully acknowledge the part these special people have played in helping me complete this book.

My wife (and best supporter), Kathy, and my two sons, Aaron and Jordan, have sacrificially and joyfully released me for the many hundreds of hours of study and writing this book required. Without their support and encouragement I would not have been free to finish. My family, especially my mother and father, have been enthusiastic cheerleaders throughout my ministry.

I want to give special honor to my pastor, mentor, uncle and spiritual father, Dr. Emanuele Cannistraci. It was largely his excellent oversight and instruction during the past two decades that have shaped my ministry. Many of the concepts of apostleship in these pages have been made real to me through watching his life.

My entire staff and congregation are super; they have supported this project since its inception. The tireless intercessors at Evangel Christian Fellowship helped me cross the finish line. My personal assistant, Sharon Gregory, has been an irreplaceable support to me, especially in editing and preparing the manuscripts.

Many friends in ministry gave me valuable input, such as Ed Delph, Cindy Jacobs and Ted Haggard. My special friend and teacher, Peter Wagner, has been a key encourager in this project. His input and inspiration have fueled the completion of this book in a significant way.

What a blessing he is to many!

Special thanks also to the people at Regal Books, who have prayed for me and have taken a courageous step in publishing this book. Regal is truly a remarkable group. Thanks to Kyle Duncan and Bayard Taylor for their feedback and editorial suggestions.

I sincerely thank God for each one of you.

INTRODUCTION

I WILL NEVER FORGET THE DAY I FIRST FELT IMPRESSED TO STUDY APOSTLES. I was in Florida at a Christian conference center and had some rare time on my hands. I had taken some training, and was scheduled to minister in some services later that week. Away from my church, my wife and my two sons, and with little to distract me, I decided that I would read the entire book of Acts.

As I read, every time I came across the word "apostle" or "apostles," I became absolutely fascinated with another aspect of their activities. I noticed that apostles did things in certain ways, and enjoyed tremendous results. Patterns began to form in my mind. *Someone needs to do a complete study on apostles,* I mused. *The Church needs to come back to some of these patterns.* The more I read, the deeper the sense of awe and wonderment grew in my spirit. I found myself in tears more than once in that little guest room. Soon I was aware of God calling me to a search for truth that would eventually become the book you hold in your hands right now.

Have you ever tried to avoid God's promptings? I tried to get several other people to write this book. Many excuses came to my mind during those first few weeks of writing. I thought I did not have the qualifications to tackle such an important subject. I pastor a wonderful congregation, I have served as a missionary in the Philippines, have managed to earn a few degrees in theology and I'm active in the leadership of our network of churches, but would people listen to me? What would I do with such a book anyway when it was completed? Yet the impression remained so strong that I knew I needed to act.

As I studied and prayed, I realized some incredible things about what God seems to be doing around the world. We are living in a truly remarkable hour. Everywhere you turn, the Kingdom is coming alive with newness and excitement. Something is in the air. I began to believe that *part* of that "something" is a renewal of the apostolic ministry.

God promised that prior to the second coming of Christ, a restoration would occur—a setting back in order—within the Church:

> Whom heaven must receive until the times of restoration of all things, which God has spoken by the mouth of all His holy prophets since the world began (Acts 3:21).

During the past four centuries, we have seen this restoration of the Church gradually unfold. We have recovered many of the critical truths and experiences that were lost in the darkness of the Middle Ages. Through Martin Luther, for example, we have recovered the message and experience of justification by faith. Because of men such as George Whitefield and John Wesley, we have come back to the truths of holiness in the Church.

In the twentieth century, we have seen similar restorations of divine healing, the gifts of the Spirit and a renewal in praise and worship. Many believe we are in the midst of the greatest worldwide revival of prayer in history. It is awe inspiring to consider how quickly the Church is returning to New Testament dynamism.

As a part of this process of restoration, we have seen a partial rebirth of the gift ministries of Ephesians 4:11 within the Church (i.e., apostles, prophets, evangelists, pastors and teachers). In the 1950s, the Body of Christ was flooded with evangelists, and in the '60s and '70s the ministries of pastors and teachers seemed to come into their own in the worldwide Body of Christ. In the '80s, we witnessed the beginnings of a remarkable openness to the widespread operation of the prophetic ministry. One office has yet to be restored in the same measure the other ministries have enjoyed, and I believe it is a missing link in the chain of restoration: *We still need the office of the apostle to manifest in its fullness.*

After that watershed moment at the Florida conference center, I soon realized that, according to Paul's pattern of the Church, only when this ministry also functions freely can we come to the unity of the faith, and only then can we mature to the full stature of Christ (see Eph. 4:13). Because the unity of the Church is essential (not to mention the maturing of the saints), this seemed to further underscore the importance of the study of apostles.

We must have unity, and we must return to the kind of power the Early Church had if we plan to complete the Great Commission. To fulfill these priorities, we must see the gift of apostleship restored and added to a place of prominence equal to the other gifts.

My investigation led me to discover that many in the Body of Christ sense that the apostolic ministry is the next ministry God will begin to restore. Could it be that now, at the dawn of a new millennium, the apostle is being reborn, and that a great worldwide movement of apostles is about to mature?

If this is so, we need the specific direction, revelation and preparation that His Word provides us. We need to answer some tough questions: *What is an apostle? How does an apostle function in the Church? What will the apostolic movement consist of?* These are the questions faced and answered in these pages.

I am aware that the message of this book may stir some debate. As a charismatic, I know that some of my positions will be slightly different from the teachings of other streams in the evangelical community, and I certainly did not write this book to polarize people. I do not presume to have the final say on any of these matters. I'm really hoping to help kick off a dialogue that can bring us all together around the apostolic paradigm found in the New Testament. I believe that what God wants to do involves all of us, whether we are from charismatic, fundamental or other backgrounds.

Certain apprehensions could be evoked by this kind of a book as well. For example, as I aim the spotlight on apostles, it may appear to some that I am dimming the lights on other ministries. Let me say from the beginning that I do not believe apostles are *more* important than any other ministry offices such as pastors or teachers, but I believe they are *as* important. Further, without the restoration of apostles, other ministries will be incomplete. Now is the time for us to simply bring apostles into focus in the Body of Christ and to include them in the spotlight along with the other essential gifts Christ has given us.

Others may feel that I am advocating that undue authority be given to modern apostles, and that I would endorse a wave of self-appointed men claiming to have "special" authority, or wanting to compose additional Scripture (heaven help us!). So, where necessary, I have attempted to distinguish and balance *modern apostleship* with the *unique apostleship* of the men who, for example, wrote much of the New Testament and whose functions will never be duplicated by another. These balances will be generously sprinkled throughout the book, and we need to note them to avoid problems.

It is my hope that you, dear reader, will consider these perspectives carefully, even if they are different from your own. Often balanced truth is found in the intersection of differing outlooks. Many people around the world already share these views and find them to be helpful in expanding the Church. I invite anyone who is interested in the world harvest to wade into this discussion with me, to think through these questions and to participate in examining and propagating the message of Scripture relating to balanced apostolic ministry. Whether you are a trained theologian, church leader or committed believer, it is my special prayer that as you read, your place in the destiny of the Church—and the present worldwide renewal—will be revealed more fully by the Spirit of God.

AN APOSTOLIC WAVE IS COMING!

JUST THE THOUGHT OF IT IS INCREDIBLE: A NEW MILLENNIUM IS UPON US. As of the year A.D. 2000, *we will again become a first-century Church!* Where is the Church of Jesus Christ in relation to the first-century Church of two thousand years ago? What does the future hold for God's people?

We live in a challenging world that is ripe for a move of the Spirit. The standards of morality in most nations are disintegrating to new lows. The traditional family is eroding. Financial markets threaten to crumble. Wars and a new round of terrorist attacks rip at the innocent, while governments are strangely aligning with a New World order. Plagues and famines are widespread. Just living takes courage.

Amid these trends, the American Church appears largely fragmented, anemic and struggling to recapture its part of the Great Commission: preaching the gospel to every nation and discipling all who believe (see Matt. 28:19). True, we are seeing incredible results in Asia, Latin America and Africa, but despite these exciting developments, after two thousand years, the fact remains that we have not yet completed our assignment.

How does God view the Church at this hour? World conditions are no surprise to Him, nor is the state of the Body of Christ. His plan brings a solution for the crises—and opportunities—of this critical hour. Now more than ever, God's people need to understand His perspective on the Church in a world at the dawn of a new millennium—a perspective that integrates hope for the future with a promise from yesterday.

THE DAMSEL IS NOT DEAD!

In Mark 5, we read the story of an encounter between the Lord and a man named Jairus. Though his daughter was at the point of death, Jairus knew if Jesus came, she would live. By the time Jesus arrived with Jairus at his house where his daughter was waiting, the bystanders had broken the news to him that the damsel was already dead and it was too late for her to recover. Jesus had a radically different view of the situation: "The damsel is not dead, but sleepeth" (v. 39, *KJV*). Despite the mockery of the crowd, Jesus spoke a life-giving command: "Damsel,...arise" (v. 41, *KJV*). Immediately, she rose up and walked. Jesus then instructed her family to feed her.

This account can be viewed as an encouraging prophetic picture of the Church in the final moments of the twentieth century. The damsel can be seen as a portrait of the Body of Christ, who *seems* to be lying at the point of death. Many in the United States are saying that the Church has little hope of recovery; others are proclaiming that the Church there is already dead.

Jesus, however, is actively building His Church around the world and has an entirely different view of things. The Church is not dead, especially in many Third World nations such as Korea, Brazil, Argentina and the Philippines. In the United States, it is as though we have been asleep and a living Christ is now awakening us by His power. He is speaking a new life-giving command to His people today:

> Arise, shine; for your light has come! And the glory of the Lord is risen upon you. For behold, the darkness shall cover the earth, and deep darkness the people; but the Lord will arise over you, and His glory will be seen upon you (Isa. 60:1,2).

There is still life in us. Like the damsel, our most exciting years are yet ahead. By His life-giving touch and some solid food, the Church is going to arise and change the world.

THE FIRST APOSTOLIC WAVE

When the disciples received the Holy Spirit at Pentecost, a massive wave of God's power hit the earth. People were overwhelmed with the dynamic outpouring of spiritual power. Crowds poured into the middle of the street. Civil and religious authorities tried to control what was already uncontrollable. Peter defined it: God's Spirit was being poured out on all flesh.

> "For these are not drunk, as you suppose, since it is only the third hour of the day. But this is what was spoken by the prophet Joel: 'And it shall come to pass in the last days, says God, that I will pour out of My Spirit on all flesh; your sons and your daughters shall prophesy, your young men shall see visions, your old men shall dream dreams. And on My menservants and on My maidservants I will pour out My Spirit in those days; and they shall prophesy. I will show wonders in heaven above and signs in the earth beneath: blood and fire and vapor of smoke. The sun shall be turned into darkness, and the moon into blood, before the coming of the great and awesome day of the Lord. And it shall come to pass that whoever calls on the name of the Lord shall be saved'" (Acts 2:15-21).

Peter's remarks go on in Acts 2 to indicate that there would be a continuation of this outpouring in the generations to come: "For the promise is to you and to your children, and to all who are afar off, as many as the Lord our God will call" (v. 39). Peter declared what they were experiencing—God's Spirit was being poured out in fulfillment of prophecy. He also confirmed the glorious fact that the promise of Joel was for *future generations* as well. Additional outpourings of the Spirit were coming, and the results would parallel the Day of Pentecost.

The result of the first apostolic wave was awesome. God's Spirit had invaded the world and the Church was born. For the first time in history, apostolic men, changed by the power of God, preached the gospel with a holy intensity. Miracles were wrought publicly. Mass repentance and dramatic conversions followed. Cities were transformed and darkness was driven back. And for decades afterward, entire regions shook under the influence of the Spirit of God with similar results, until the apostles gained the reputation of being those through whom the known world was turned upside down (see 17:6).

The late William Steuart McBirnie, a church historian and noted scholar, wrote:

> Within the lifetime of the Apostles the gospel of Christ had spread over the long Roman roads, as well as by the sea, to such far off places as Gaul and Britain to the northwest, Alexandria and Carthage on the coast of Africa to the south, Scythia and Armenia [in what is now the former Soviet Union!] to the north and Persia and India to the east. In the course of this initial outburst of Christian fervor, the Twelve Apostles, and many others also called apostles, carried the Christian message to great extremes of distance and into perilous lands both near and far, even beyond the Roman Empire. There they died, but their message and the churches they founded survived them.[1]

The first apostolic wave crashed into history, and in a very short span of time the world became a very different place.

THE APOSTOLIC SPIRIT

One of the things we will learn in this book is that the Spirit of God is an Apostolic Spirit; His nature and personality are apostolic. The New Testament word "apostle" means "sent one." God's Spirit has been sent to us (see Gal. 4:6), but there is something else to consider. *The result of the Spirit of God being poured out was an activation of true apostolic ministry, which tells us that the Spirit who generated these results must Himself be apostolic.* The Spirit of God, in His character and personality, is supernatural, invasive and life changing, and when He is poured out we can expect to see apostolic results: miracles, invasions of His work and changed lives.

Although the first move of the Apostolic Spirit was remarkable, we must not forget that other moves, according to Peter, were coming. As we have seen, the promise of outpouring was not only to the generation of believers at Pentecost, but also to generations yet to come. Looking at history, we do see that subsequent moves of the Spirit of God have come. For example, think of the wonderful things God did during the Reformation, the Great Awakenings in the United States, the

Evangelical Revival in England and the Pentecostal and charismatic movements of this century. None of them, however, entirely matches the outpouring of the Spirit as it was at Pentecost. We have read great reports in church history of these kinds of visitations, particularly within the last 150 years, but something greater is surely set for the future.

An end-time move of God is coming that will eclipse all other revivals in history. Robert E. Coleman, a noted evangelical author, agrees when he writes, "It is possible to discern an outline of a future movement of revival that will make anything seen thus far pale by comparison."[2] *Another spiritual wave is about to come across the earth, and it will be the greatest wave ever.*

THE PRESENT APOSTOLIC WAVE

Many sense that at present this wave is mounting, that the Church is already tasting the firstfruits of another massive end-time revival. An explosion of apostolic proportion is hitting the world. We are living in the first moments of a turning tide within the Church, and like the first wave, this wave will shape our new millennium.

As evidence, consider the facts. The rate at which the Church is growing in this century is explosive. The impossible things for which we interceded only a decade ago are changing before our very eyes. It is common knowledge that the destruction of the Berlin Wall and the dissolution of the U.S.S.R. caused the gospel to pour freely into Russia and the former Soviet states. What looked hopeless in sub-Saharan Africa during the rise of Islam has now reversed itself as Christianity has become the dominant spiritual force there. The icy resistance to Christ that has been real in England is melting under the fire of widespread renewal.

Reports from behind the Bamboo Curtain in China and in other parts of Asia state that multiplied thousands of believers are added to the Church daily. Latin America is presently experiencing an explosive and seemingly perpetual revival. In Korea, Buddha is bowing to the lordship of Jesus Christ as Christianity steadily grows to become the most pervasive spiritual power. Surely other nations are about to experience similar visitations.

The church-growth data for the last decade is equally encouraging. About 275 million committed and active Christians were reported worldwide in 1980. Since that time, reliable estimates point to a wave of conversions worldwide totaling some 80,000 souls coming to Christ every day, and a minimum of 20,000 of them are converting daily behind the Bamboo Curtain of Communist China![3] We must understand that these figures alone far exceed the initial conversions of the early decades of the church after Pentecost and the rapid spread of the gospel in the first century.[4] The present apostolic wave already towers over the first!

The initial phases of the present apostolic wave have placed incredible opportunities within our reach. For the first time in history, missiologists are of the mind that we have all the necessary resources—spiritual, financial and human—to fulfill the Great Commission by the end of this decade! David Shibley, a missionary statesman, heralds, "Something historic is happening. All across the world Christians are sensing that this is God's hour for global harvest. Every major stream of Christendom is pointing toward the year 2000 as a target for fulfilling Christ's Great Commission. The converging of events and people toward completing the task is unprecedented."[5]

The present wave of the Apostolic Spirit already dwarfs anything the apostles could have seen or imagined in the first apostolic movement. It seems we are entering into a visitation of greater proportion than Pentecost, and it is exactly as Joel said it would be (see Joel 2:28,29). The Holy Spirit is crashing into history again, only this time He is coming upon our generation!

This wave will reactivate true apostolic ministry for the harvest. Because the Spirit is being poured out, and because He is an Apostolic Spirit, apostles and an apostolic movement *must* result.

It appears that the hour is ripe for the emergence of a movement of modern-day apostles. John Dawson declares emphatically that "it is now a season for the restored prominence of the ministry of apostles."[6] These are the days that Bill Hamon, a leading prophet in the Church, foresaw a decade ago when he trumpeted:

> The 1990s will be the decade for the apostle. The full restoration of the apostle in the '90s will bring a restoration of full apostolic authority and the signs and wonders of the gift of faith and the working of miracles. The Christ-ordained office and ministry of the apostle will be recognized, accepted and magnified mightily throughout the Christian world.[7]

UNDERSTANDING THE STAGES
OF THE FINAL HARVEST

How will this wave culminate? When will we see the fullness of the restoration of the office of the apostle and the ensuing apostolic movement? Jesus, when teaching about the harvest and the moving of the Spirit of God, revealed a relevant principle to us in Mark 4:

> And He said, "The kingdom of God is as if a man should scatter seed on the ground, and should sleep by night and rise by day, and the seed should sprout and grow, he himself does not know how. For the earth yields crops by itself: first the blade, then the head, after that the full grain in the head. But when the grain ripens, immediately he puts in the sickle, *because the harvest has come*" (vv. 26-29, emphasis mine).

For two thousand years, spiritual seed has been sown by the Church, the gospel has been preached and martyrs have offered their lives as the ultimate seed. Jesus said these precious seeds would spring up in the earth suddenly and without explanation, and their appearance would manifest in discernible phases: "First the blade, then the head, after that the full grain in the head" (v. 28).

In terms of the present apostolic movement, we now seem to be at the blade stage, getting ready to see the ear of fruit and looking forward to the full manifestation and maturity of the harvest. Discerning harvest-watcher Cindy Jacobs predicts, "In the decade of the '90s a great harvest will be reaped."[8] We are feeling only the initial forces of this awesome current of the Spirit; most of the power lies just ahead of us. James promises us that just prior to the harvest, a latter rain of God's Spirit will fall (see Joel 2:28; compare to Jas. 5:17,18). An outpouring is coming that will usher in the harvest.

THE APOSTOLIC MOVEMENT
APPEARS CERTAIN

Several reasons help us assert that a worldwide apostolic movement is upon us:

1. *God is progressively restoring the Church to its New Testament pattern.* This pattern involves pastors, teachers, evangelists and prophets, but will not be complete until the apostle is fully restored (see Eph. 4:11). At this point, apostles are a missing link in the chain of ministry God has designed to operate in the Body of Christ.
2. *The apostle is needed until the Body reaches maturity* (see v. 13). Few would argue that we have arrived. It is illogical to think God would hold back apostles at this critical season, especially considering the vital role they played in expanding the Early Church.
3. *We can see it happening already.* As we have seen, exciting things are happening as the Church is stepping out in apostolic dimensions around the world.

CLARIFYING THE TERMS

Before we go forward with the effort to identify the details of the apostolic movement and the ministry of apostles, it will help if we clarify some key terms.

What is an apostle? Throughout the history of the Church, the title "apostle" has been used in various ways to mean a variety of things. For example, the title has referred to the "twelve apostles" Jesus appointed (see Matt. 10:2-4). In the evangelical Protestant tradition, influenced by cessationist theology*, apostleship is usually restricted to these twelve with perhaps a few exceptions. In chapter 4, we will make a strong case for the existence of many apostles in the New Testament *outside the twelve*, including such noteworthy apostles as Paul and Barnabas.

The term "apostle" has also been used to refer to the leaders of the first Christian missions to a country, such as Saint Patrick of Ireland or Saint Cyril of the Slavs. These men, and many other church-planting pioneers, are rightly seen as apostles by the Church because they have been responsible for spreading Christianity into foreign lands, just as the biblical apostles were.

---

*Cessationists argue (using 1 Corinthians 13:8-10 and John 16:13) that the charismatic gifts described in the Epistles and Acts ceased in the first century and were replaced by the canon of the New Testament Scripture. Please refer to chapter 12 for my position on cessationism.

In the Roman Catholic, Eastern Orthodox and Episcopal traditions, the term "apostle" is usually associated with *apostolic succession*, the doctrine that the grace and authority of Christ has descended from the original twelve apostles through their lawfully appointed successors, or bishops. Protestants have generally disputed the claim of apostolic succession because it relies more on extrabiblical church tradition than on the clear interpretation of Scripture.

Various other fairly common uses of the word "apostle" or "apostolic" are as follows: Since the seventeenth century the first generation of church leaders after the New Testament have been labeled "the Apostolical Fathers"; the most widely accepted affirmation of faith among Christians is the "Apostles' Creed"; one of the most popular orders of worship in Eastern Orthodox churches and the Roman Catholic church is the "Apostolic tradition"; and many Protestants interpret the gift of *apostle* as *missionary*.

Our definition, however, is somewhat different. In this book, we are defining an "apostle" as one who is called and sent by Christ to have the spiritual authority, character, gifts and abilities to successfully reach and establish people in Kingdom truth and order, especially through founding and overseeing local churches.

Other definitions are important as well: *Apostolic people* are Christians who support and participate in apostolic ministry, but are not actual apostles. Apostolic people work with apostles to reach the lost through dynamic outreach, church planting and nurturing. *Apostolic churches* are churches that recognize and relate to modern-day apostles and are active in varying forms of apostolic ministry. *The apostolic movement* is the Holy Spirit's worldwide activation of apostles and apostolic people to come together as a part of a great revival on earth. Throughout this book, we will be further explaining these terms and how they relate to what God is doing today.

The reader might well ask in this connection: Are apostles all that important? As we shall see, a restored function of New Testament apostles is not only *important*, but it is also *critical*. Apostles are first in the ministry of the Church (see 1 Cor. 12:28). Apostles are an essential part of the team God has formed so the Church can be built up (see Eph. 4:11-17). Apostles are the wise master builders God has given so the Church can be properly built (see 1 Cor. 3:10). Without the apostle, the team is incomplete, and the church cannot be properly built. I truly believe that as we return to the biblical patterns of apostles and apostolic people, we will quickly move closer to the revived New Testament church that is needed at this hour.

THE PURPOSE OF THIS BOOK

What should we do in light of all these things? We must respond with wisdom and passion, moving together in the same direction as God's Spirit, fully aware of His plan for the consummation of this age. Those who fail to appreciate and participate in this movement will miss what may shape up to be the greatest opportunity in the history of the Church.

The purpose of this book is to alert the Body of Christ to the fact that a great apostolic blade is springing up in our midst, and is developing into an exciting manifestation of its ministry. Scriptural and prophetic truths will help the Body of Christ be aware of the apostolic movement's nature and purpose. We need encouragement and direction in how to flow with this movement, and guidelines and inspiration for the vast number who are called to become the new generation of apostles and apostolic people.

The Church is alive and ready to shine. As at Pentecost, God's Spirit is being poured out again today with exciting results. What else could account for the progress we are making in so many countries, as we have seen? This second great wave of the Spirit, now in the early stages of advancement, will culminate in nothing short of the final harvest of the earth. Another sparkling rush from His presence is washing over the earth, only this time the results will be greater, just as Christ prophesied:

> "Most assuredly, I say to you, he who believes in Me, the works that I do he will do also; and greater works than these he will do, because I go to My Father" (John 14:12).

The world is waiting and ready for God to move. The Church is awakening, and, as it was at Pentecost, God is sending forth His power to change history. When it is finished, a trail of apostolic exploits will be left behind, God's plan will be fulfilled and the harvest will be reaped. Because He is sending His Spirit now, we must receive the wonderful work He is doing and *catch this exciting wave.*

Notes

1. William Steuart McBirnie, *The Search for the Twelve Apostles* (Wheaton, Ill.: Tyndale House, 1978), p. 38.
2. Ralph D. Winter and Steven C. Hawthorne, eds., *Perspectives on the World Christian Movement* (Pasadena: The William Carey Library, 1992), p. B-220.
3. C. Peter Wagner, "New Equipment for the Final Thrust," *Ministries Today* (January/February 1994): 28.
4. Ibid.
5. David Shibley, *A Force in the Earth* (Altamonte Springs, Fla.: Creation House, 1989), pp. 13-14.
6. John Dawson, *Taking Our Cities for God* (Lake Mary, Fla.: Creation House, 1989), p. 11.
7. Bill Hamon, *Prophets and the Prophetic Movement* (Shippensburg, Pa.: Destiny Image, 1990), p. 49.
8. Cindy Jacobs, *Possessing the Gates of the Enemy* (Grand Rapids: Chosen Books, 1991), p. 68.

2

CATCHING THE WAVE

MY FAMILY AND I LOVE THE BALMY WEATHER, PRISTINE BEACHES AND AZURE waters of the Hawaiian Islands. Some of our greatest memories are of days spent together, playfully relaxing and enjoying the sun.

On many such occasions, I have watched the amazing skill of the local people as they surf. Using a combination of intuition and experience, they paddle out on their colorful boards to just the right spot on the water, carefully positioning themselves in relation to the approaching wave. Usually there is a brief moment of suspense, and then, quite suddenly, they rise up on their boards with a balance and beauty that seems to defy natural laws. Mounting up and forward as they go, they are carried along triumphantly toward the shore by the curling surf. This is called *catching the wave*, and it is an inspiring sight.

The Church today is in the same position as a surfer waiting for a wave. God is preparing us now for an awesome movement of the Spirit. Our timing and posture are vital and our success depends on position and anticipation. Although it is exciting to know that a wave of God's Spirit is arising, it is essential that we be fully positioned to *catch it* as it comes.

In this chapter, we will view the coming apostolic wave by using prophetic eyes: what it will look like, how we can catch it and where it will take us.

At Pentecost, the first wave spilled out into the streets, villages and nations, quickly overtaking the world. It was like the wave that breaks and furiously spreads out upon itself and the beach, stretching out over the surface of the earth. The coming apostolic wave will be similar. After the earth feels the thunder of its crash, there will be a rapid distribution of the apostles and apostolic people born in the movement until the earth is covered and its presence is felt everywhere.

WHAT WILL THE APOSTOLIC MOVEMENT BE?

Throughout the remainder of this book, the focus will be on developing an understanding of the key ingredients of the emerging apostolic movement. In general, it will be measured in four important dimensions.

1. Restoring the New Testament Office of the Apostle

A complete manifestation of the scriptural apostolic function within the worldwide Body of Christ will occur. John Calvin, the reformer, was accurate when he said of apostles that the Lord "now and again revives them as the need of the time demands."[1] Never has the need of the times demanded a greater manifestation of the apostolic ministry. The nations will be visited by a new company of apostles who will function as the apostles of the Early Church did. This will constitute a new generation of *apostolic pacesetters*. The number of these apostles cannot be known, but given the task of taking the nations in the final harvest, it is likely that they will number into the thousands.

In chapter 6, we will address the question: "What Is an Apostle?" in detail, and then in later chapters we will develop these ideas. We will look at the work of an apostle in "Planting and Watering for Increase" (chapter 7), the heart of an apostle in "The Signs of an Apostle" (chapter 8), and Satan's counterfeit of true apostles, "False Apostles" (chapter 10). Other chapters will help us complete the picture of the true ministry of an apostle as it will manifest in this movement.

2. Imparting Christ's Apostolic Anointing

The anointing of Christ the apostle (see Heb. 3:1) will refresh and activate the Church. Apostles figure centrally in the plan of God for this hour, but they will not function alone. The apostle is given by Christ to equip, mature and activate the people of God (see Eph. 4:11,12), making us an *apostolic people*. In this book, we are exploring the place that people who are not called to be apostles can play in the world harvest and, as mentioned before, we are identifying them as apostolic people. As we shall discover, anyone who is sent by God is apostolic, even if the person is not an apostle.

The Spirit of God will be poured out to empower the process of multiplying apostolic people and apostolic churches. This will constitute a tangible visitation of God within His people, and will likely attract great attention. Most important, the Body of Christ will become focused, sensitive and committed to reaching planet Earth as never before. In chapter 4, we will concentrate on developing the concept of "Changing the World Through Apostolic People." This is one of the most exciting aspects of the apostolic movement.

3. A Dramatic Revival of Supernatural Signs, Wonders and Miracles

If we plan to see the office of the apostle restored and an outpouring of the apostolic anointing on the Body, it follows that we will also witness the kinds of miracles and signs that followed the first-century apostles. As we shall learn in chapter 8, "The Signs of an Apostle," and in chapter 12, "Apostles and Supernatural Power," a crystal clear correlation between the ministry of apostles in the New Testament and the supernatural dimension exists. Ultimately, *apostolic pacesetters and apostolic people* will walk in *apostolic power*. The sick shall be healed, and the oppressed will be delivered in large numbers. As a result, many will be converted and the light of the gospel will overtake the darkness of the world.

4. A Worldwide Deployment of Thousands of Apostles

The apostles will be strategically deployed as the Spirit of God speaks to them about cities and nations to be reached. The deployment will transcend groups, denominational boards and agencies, and will not be the work of any one organization. Many modern "Macedonian calls" will be made (see Acts 16:9,10). The Spirit of God will speak at prophetic gatherings about individual callings, and apostles will be sent out as at Antioch (see Acts 13:1-3). Thousands will take their places in the final thrust of world evangelization through this life-changing *apostolic positioning*. Each apostle will be unique, but will walk in the patterns of the Early Church apostles, traveling, strategically ministering and building the kingdom of God.

To summarize, *the apostolic movement will consist of a company of apostolic pacesetters who demonstrate apostolic power and lead apostolic people into apostolic positions all over the world.*

CAN THIS WORK IN OUR CHURCH?

Throughout the process of preparing this book, I have enjoyed talking to people from historical, fundamental and noncharismatic theological backgrounds about the subject of modern-day apostles. Not surprisingly, I have found an increasing openness to apostles among many of them. I believe this to be true for two reasons:

1. It is clear that God is preparing the whole Church, not just one part of the Church, to be used in this exciting move of the Spirit. After all, we are one Body, and God doesn't have any favorite children.

2. An in-depth study of modern apostles is quite convincing. We all believe in missionaries, who throughout history have served as the apostles of their day, though not always by that name. Whether or not we call them apostles or missionaries, we cannot overlook the invaluable contribution of people such as Zinzendorf and the Moravians, William Carey in India, Hudson Taylor in China, the Puritans, the Pietists or the many thousands of others throughout the history of the Church who have spread the gospel and established churches. No one could deny that such ministries are needed today in large number. Considering the insight we have into the area of apostolic ministry, I believe many principles outlined here could be profitably transferred to what is now regarded as missionary work.

Furthermore, what we call the fivefold ministry gifts of Ephesians 4:11 is not a purely Pentecostal or charismatic paradigm. It is a biblical pattern that the whole Body of Christ can, and must, utilize. We are not far afield. In the charismatic arm of the Church, evangelists, pastors and teachers are as common as they are in the noncharismatic. Prophetic ministries are being widely accepted, especially in the charismatic church. Missionaries are a part of both theological frameworks. We are getting close.

To be sure, some tangible differences still exist in our theological grids. I cannot accurately predict how much of this will change, or when it will change. The obvious goal in Scripture is that "we all come to the unity of the faith" (Eph. 4:13). We now need to allow the Lord to stretch us and pull us together around the patterns of His Word. I truly believe He is doing that already. By some careful study, open dialogue and fervent prayer, the apostolic movement can flourish among people from any church tradition.

A SPIRITUALLY BIRTHED MOVEMENT

How will this mighty visitation manifest itself? Before we can comprehend the details of this movement and the ministry it will bring into prominence, we must build a base of understanding that will enable us to grasp the fullness of what God wants to do. I'd like to present two simple analogies I believe will help us. The dual pictures of a *wave* and a *birth* will illustrate some important dimensions of the emerging apostolic movement.

Because a powerful apostolic wave was released on the earth at the birth of the Church, we have a wonderful pattern by which we can begin to anticipate the present wave. Because the first wave birthed the Church, it is fitting that we view the present wave as another birth; not another birth of the Church, as at Pentecost, but another birth *within* the Church. This movement will constitute a wonderful rebirth of God's apostolic power within the Body of Christ.

All spiritual births are the result of relationship. In Romans 7, the believer's relationship with Christ is pictured as a powerful union ultimately resulting in a glorious spiritual birth. This principle forms the foundation of an understanding of the birthing of any real spiritual life in God's people. Consider this wonderful spiritual picture:

> Or do you not know, brethren (for I speak to those who know the law), that the law has dominion over a man as long as he lives? For the woman who has a husband is bound by the law to her husband as long as he lives. But if the husband dies, she is released from the law of her husband. So then if, while her husband lives, she marries another man, she will be called an adulteress; but if her hus-

band dies, she is free from that law, so that she is no adul-
teress, though she has married another man. Therefore, my
brethren, you also have become dead to the law through the
body of Christ, that you may be married to another—to
Him who was raised from the dead, that we should bear
fruit to God. For when we were in the flesh, the sinful passions which were aroused by the law were at work in our
members to bear fruit to death. But now we have been
delivered from the law, having died to what we were held
by, so that we should serve in the newness of the Spirit and
not in the oldness of the letter (Rom. 7:1-6).

Following in chapter 8, Paul alludes to the *process* of spiritual
birthing, which involves the groaning and travail of intercession. As
Cindy Jacobs has pointed out, "The spirit of prayer that comes upon
nations and people actually constitutes the birth pangs of revival."[2]
Notice the truths of travail and birthing, which also shape our understanding of God's Spirit moving among His people:

For we know that the whole creation groans and labors
with birth pangs together until now. Not only that, but we
also who have the firstfruits of the Spirit, even we ourselves groan within ourselves, eagerly waiting for the
adoption, the redemption of our body. For we were saved
in this hope, but hope that is seen is not hope; for why does
one still hope for what he sees? But if we hope for what we
do not see, we eagerly wait for it with perseverance.
Likewise the Spirit also helps in our weaknesses. For we do
not know what we should pray for as we ought, but the
Spirit Himself makes intercession for us with groanings
which cannot be uttered. Now He who searches the hearts
knows what the mind of the Spirit is, because He makes
intercession for the saints according to the will of God
(Rom. 8:22-27).

When our relationship with Christ is viewed through Paul's alle-
gories of marriage and childbirth, fascinating dimensions of truth
develop. As we desire to peek into the process of the birthing of the

next apostolic move, we gain light by looking through the allegory of the bride of Christ and her heavenly groom.

In any relationship, a natural order of progression develops in ever-increasing levels of intimacy until a birth occurs. What about our relationship with Jesus? How might the same truth apply?

THE PROCESS OF NEW LIFE

The human process of marriage begins with *courtship*, where a pursuit is made by the man to engage the woman and her affections. When I first met my wife, Kathy, I was only 14 years old. We were at an all-night prayer meeting in our church, which then was still small and mainly consisted of young people. When I first saw Kathy, my focus on prayer was significantly hindered! I knew then that this was a girl I wanted to get to know better. I chose to pursue a relationship with her, and I am, of course, very glad I did. That was back in 1974, and we have had many wonderful experiences together since then. It all started with a young man pursuing his bride-to-be.

In the same way, Christ has sought us and chosen us for Himself. Jesus said, "You did not choose Me, but I chose you and appointed you that you should go and bear fruit, and that your fruit should remain, that whatever you ask the Father in My name He may give you" (John 15:16). How marvelous it is to know that Jesus loves His people and pursues intimacy with them that results in new life!

The next step in a natural relationship is *marriage*, where the two are joined in covenant love. My relationship with Kathy progressed until we were married: a commitment was made, and Kathy became my precious bride. According to Paul's allegory, believers are married to Christ. We are the bride of Christ (see Eph. 5:23-32; Rev. 21:2,9; 22:17). The deep love and affection of our relationship with Christ is wrapped up in a blanket of security and a permanency based upon covenant promises.

Does it stop there? The next step in the natural relationship is *intimacy* between the bride and bridegroom. This comes only after covenant love is established, and is necessary for bringing forth birth. The implication in Paul's allegory is that this union is one of intimate relationship. Intimacy between the people of God and the Lord Jesus is an essential part of our lives, and is the basis of all our activities with God.

After intimacy comes *conception*, when the seed finds a place in the innermost being and new life begins. Kathy and I have two wonderful sons who came into our lives as a result of conception following intimacy. In our relationship with the Lord, His Word becomes a seed sown deep within us to release new life. Mary became an instrument through which God was able to bring the life of Jesus. In a similar way, when we come into intimacy with Christ, the life of Jesus comes alive within us.

Gestation—a long period of gradual and hidden development—follows conception. We must remember that birthing is not an overnight process. As my wife will quickly tell you, discomfort is felt at this stage. Nothing seems to fit or feel right. Yet the miraculous processes of gestation are building up strength and vitality within. Similarly, whenever the bride of Christ receives the Word and new life is conceived within us, a period of uncomfortable waiting follows in which the Word matures.

When the process of gestation is complete, the bride anticipates the arrival of the new life, but it cannot manifest until an intense and painful process known as travail comes to draw the new life into the world. Paul likens travail to the Spirit of God intensively praying through us so that a spiritual birth may result (see Rom. 8:22-27; Gal. 4:19). When God's people allow travailing prayer to come upon them, they are not far from the manifestation of a new move of God.

The final result is birth. This brings the new life to the earth, and causes great rejoicing. Jesus said: "A woman, when she is in labor, has sorrow because her hour has come; but as soon as she has given birth to the child, she no longer remembers the anguish, for joy that a human being has been born into the world" (John 16:21). Just as any parent rejoices in the birth of a new son or daughter, our relationship with Christ produces incredible joy as new life comes forth!

THE BIRTH OF THE APOSTOLIC MOVEMENT

Why have we focused on this allegory? Because we need to see that in the birth of this visitation, certain signals will go off in sequence to mark the development of the apostolic movement. It is important that we be able to identify where we are in the process of God's activity on the earth.

We can look for a new intimacy in the relationship between Christ and His bride, drawing us into the conception and gestation of a new life in the Church. One sign of any move of God is a renewal of worship in the Church, revealing relational intimacy. This intimacy draws us close to Him, close enough to hear His very heartbeat for the world. Then we are ready for the seed of His Word saying: "Let the apostles arise." Once that seed takes hold within us, we are forever changed. Gestation may make us uncomfortable, and it may try our patience, but our reward will be in seeing the actual fruit being born as a glorious new moving of God's presence on the earth. Just prior to the full revelation of this move, we will see a period of intense intercession and travail, as Zion brings forth a new dimension of life.

> Who has heard such a thing? Who has seen such things? Shall the earth be made to give birth in one day? Or shall a nation be born at once? For as soon as Zion was in labor, she gave birth to her children (Isa. 66:8).

THE MANIFESTATION OF A MOVEMENT

When the fruit of this union comes forth, what will it look like? The question can be answered in two senses: first, it is likely to be reminiscent of the outpouring at Pentecost that gave rise to the first apostolic movement; second, it will bear a striking resemblance to a wave, just as we have seen. Let's view it in the analogous language of that first wave of Pentecost.

A Swell in the Surface

Initially a natural wave comes quietly as a rolling swell in the surface of the waters, while beneath the surface, unseen forces are acting that will produce unbelievable power.

I believe the next apostolic wave will begin just as a natural wave begins. The force of the Spirit will move out of the void, just as in creation. "And the Spirit of God was hovering over the face of the waters" (Gen. 1:2). God's Spirit is brooding over the waters of the Church, unifying the Body, to raise up His mighty wave. Without that essential ingredient of unity, the power of the apostolic movement will quickly dissipate.

A Projection of Energy

At Pentecost, the believers gathered expectantly, waiting for the promise as Christ had instructed. They tarried patiently in one accord, pouring out intercession before the Lord.

A natural wave, after the swelling in the surface begins, suddenly projects as the shape of the wave rises unmistakably from the surface. Soon a curl and then a crash will occur as the churning ocean explodes upon itself.

We will see such an explosion in the next apostolic wave. As God's people rise up in an exciting new unity, direction will come and movement will be detected. Some might ask, "What will this wave mean in terms of the unity of the Body of Christ?" I cannot say for sure how it will happen, but I am certain that somehow this wave will usher in a greater organic unity in the Church. To be sure, it will be clear to all that a distinct wave is growing—that spiritual energy is gaining momentum and bringing us together, just as at Pentecost. What a time of joy that will be!

A Crest in the Wave

When the Spirit began to move on the Day of Pentecost, He appeared to the intercessors as a mighty rushing wind and a powerful lick of fire. The Spirit of God usually manifests itself progressively—like a river that begins with just a few drops and then comes crashing through the desert.

A natural wave, once the projection is upon the surface of the water, reaches the point of no return; energy builds within the wave until the top of the wave overtakes the surface and a crest is formed. Froth and mist are released as the force of the water builds pressure and momentum. Can you see it coming?

This is a picture of the coming apostolic wave at the height of its fullness. The wave will attract attention and make a resounding noise as apostles operate fully on the earth to establish churches, win the lost, penetrate darkness and display the power of the Spirit of God.

An Awesome Crash

The Spirit was poured out in an uncontrollable gush that day in the Upper Room. No one could question the life-changing quality of that spectacular moment when those gathered were baptized in the Spirit. What a thrill and awe must have come into their spirits!

In a natural wave, after the crest comes such a crash. As the noise of pounding surf thunders through the air, all the pent-up energy of the wave explodes upon itself as water arcs through the air, and the wave rolls on as uncontrollably and unpredictably as new wine.

The same will hold true as the apostolic wave crashes across the earth. It will carry an awesome force and pack an explosive nature. The culture was unable to stop the apostles in the early chapters of Acts, likewise no one will be able to stop this gushing wave of the Spirit.

A Dynamic Dispersion

At Pentecost, the power in the Upper Room did not remain inside; it spilled out into the streets, villages and nations, quickly overtaking the world like the wave that breaks and spreads out over the surface of the earth. The final stage of the apostolic wave will be similar. After the earth feels the thunder of its crash, a rapid distribution of the apostles and apostolic people born in the movement will occur until the earth is covered and its presence is felt everywhere.

How to Catch the Apostolic Wave

Getting a glimpse of the glory of this birth and the beauty of this wave awakens our desires and prompts us to consider how we can be involved. The movement by nature will seek to involve the personal participation of each member of the Body of Christ, for we are one Body. As with anything in God's kingdom, the *realization* of this visitation will be relative to the *response* of God's people. How then, should we prepare to be involved? We must be willing to make four sincere commitments.

1. *We must be receptive to what God is doing in our day.* We must be open and align ourselves with God's role in this final act of history. For many, certain aspects of this movement will cut across the religious traditions of the past. The first-century apostolic movement threatened those who did not see its origin in the Spirit of God. They persecuted it, but we must think differently. We cannot persecute, criticize or condemn the work of God. Because we have not yet won the world apart from the ministry of the apostle, it is time for the apostles to find a place of acceptance in the Body of Christ and a place of vibrant activity in the world. We must join Ed Murphy, a missionary and author, as he prays, "May God raise up thousands of such twentieth century apostles for today's Church! May He also help us recognize them when He does raise them up!"[3]

2. We must desire what God is doing. God wants to ignite a blazing spiritual passion in us. Before we can be involved, we must hunger and thirst after righteousness. This kind of anticipation positions us in a faith that receives (see Mark 11:24). Church historian and theologian Vinson Synan has already identified the existence of this type of hunger. "Among many independent charismatics, a thirst has developed for the restoration of apostolic authority in the body of Christ."[4] May it increase with every passing second!

3. We must be committed to what God is doing. If we believe that God is doing something, we will express this faith with corresponding action. Faith without action is dead (see Jas. 2:17-20). We must be involved with everything we have: our time, our talents and our treasures. The alternative is simply to be left behind.

4. We must be sensitive to the call. We have a place in God's plan. God wants His people to hear the call. Each soldier must hear His orders if we are going to win the battle. We must let God's Word direct our paths and let those in spiritual authority guide us with their counsel. We must listen for God's voice in prayer—He might be speaking to each of us today.

We are living in an awesome hour. A great wave is breaking and birthing a wonderful new life. The Spirit of God is releasing a mighty apostolic movement. We cannot afford to miss what God is doing. Another wave of apostles and apostolic people is coming forth to touch the nations, and we must be positioned to catch it. When we are properly positioned, we will be ready to fulfill the *apostolic call*.

Notes

1. Vinson Synan, "Who Are the Modern Apostles?" *Ministries Today* (March/April 1992): 45.
2. Cindy Jacobs, *Possessing the Gates of the Enemy* (Grand Rapids: Chosen Books, 1991), p. 68.
3. Ed Murphy, *Spiritual Gifts and the Great Commission* (Pasadena: William Carey Library, 1975—currently out of print), p. 235.
4. Synan, "Who Are the Modern Apostles?": 45.

THE
APOSTOLIC CALL

PETER AND ANDREW HAD HEARD THAT JESUS WAS BEGINNING TO PREACH IN their hometown of Capernaum. "Repent, for the kingdom of heaven is at hand" (Matt. 3:2; 4:17). The message itself was nothing new. John the Baptist had been preaching the same thing, and was he not now in prison for it? They had heard something about John's skirmishes.

Somehow, the words of this preacher Jesus loomed larger and more authoritative than John's. Some said He also performed miracles. Could this be the Messiah? He was causing quite a stir in the small coastal town. At any rate, they did not have time to dwell on the latest news; they had families to feed and fish to catch. They continued with business as usual, until one morning these apostles-in-the-making were confronted with the Christ. That encounter turned out to be an appointment with destiny that changed them forever.

"Follow Me, and I will make you fishers of men" (4:19). The challenge was magnetic, drawing them like so many fish in a net. What did He mean? For how long? What about the business, the bills and the boats?

Yet an awesome promise was ringing in that invitation—a change of life, a new purpose higher than anything they had known. They would be with Jesus! An innate instinct compelled them, and they purposed to follow the apostolic call. The sound of their nets dropping to the ground was barely heard in Capernaum that day, but it thundered in the heavens.

THE APOSTOLIC CALL
IS STILL GOING FORTH

Nearly two thousand years later, Jesus continues to call apostles and apostolic people. Throughout the earth today, people like Peter and Andrew are coming alive to the reality that Christ is calling them. This momentum is building in lives every day, moving us closer to the full manifestation of the apostolic movement. Today's call is as real as at any previous time for men and women to rise up and reap the nations with the Lord of the harvest. He is walking the shorelines of our comfortable lives, challenging people to respond and to be used to change lives and fulfill destiny. The question for us is: *How tightly are we holding onto our nets?*

The apostolic calling is a summons to believers that issues from the Father through Jesus. It is the voice of God alive in our spirits, saying, "Come and follow Me." It is a call for the Church to go to the nations, issued to apostles and apostolic people alike. It is both an invitation and a command to become like Christ, and to embrace His desires for the world.

The emerging apostolic movement will be built on a sharp increase of the apostolic call to serve in the Kingdom. Like an army, this new apostolic company will throw down their nets and rise at the command of the Lord of Hosts. Hearing the call, they will aggressively engage the enemy, taking his territory in the greatest campaign in history: *the evangelization of planet Earth before the second coming of the Lord Jesus.*

THE WISDOM AND POWER
OF THE APOSTOLIC CALL

The purpose of the apostolic call is to create apostles through which Christ the Apostle can function on earth, maturing a people of victory, love and Christlikeness. The apostle Paul's words describe the manner in which apostles are called by Christ to perfect the saints:

> And He Himself gave some to be apostles, some prophets, some evangelists, and some pastors and teachers, for the equipping of the saints for the work of ministry, for the edifying of the body of Christ, till we all come to the unity of

the faith and of the knowledge of the Son of God, to a perfect man, to the measure of the stature of the fullness of Christ; that we should no longer be children, tossed to and fro and carried about with every wind of doctrine, by the trickery of men, in the cunning craftiness of deceitful plotting, but, speaking the truth in love, may grow up in all things into Him who is the head—Christ—from whom the whole body, joined and knit together by what every joint supplies, according to the effective working by which every part does its share, causes growth of the body for the edifying of itself in love (Eph. 4:11-16).

According to the Lord Jesus, this eternal calling reveals the marvelous wisdom of God at work in the universe: "Therefore the wisdom of God also said, 'I will send them prophets and apostles'" (Luke 11:49).

When we see God raising up apostles in this emerging movement, we will be witnessing the reality of God's eternal wisdom working on earth. This release of wisdom will come as an offensive strike against Satan and his dark princes, further establishing the eternal purpose of God in Christ. Each time the call goes forth and is answered, darkness slips into a greater degree of defeat before the throne:

(By which, when you read, you may understand my knowledge in the mystery of Christ), which in other ages was not made known to the sons of men, as it has now been revealed by the Spirit to His holy *apostles* and prophets: that the Gentiles should be fellow heirs, of the same body, and partakers of His promise in Christ through the gospel, of which I became a minister according to the gift of the grace of God given to me by the effective working of His power. To me, who am less than the least of all the saints, this grace was given, that I should preach among the Gentiles the unsearchable riches of Christ, and to make all see what is the fellowship of the mystery, which from the beginning of the ages has been hidden in God who created all things through Jesus Christ; *to the intent that now the manifold wisdom of God might be made known by the church to the principalities and powers in the heavenly places* (Eph. 3:4-10, emphasis added).

Few have understood the magnitude of the apostle and his call from Christ. The apostle is a central part of the demonstration of the manifold wisdom of God; not only to raise the Church to maturity, but to defeat the enemy and his plan to control the earth. This is why it is essential that the apostles and apostolic people emerge as a part of the end-time events of the harvest. The apostolic call that is going forth today from Christ must be obeyed. Every time a person answers the apostolic call—every time another net drops to the ground—that person is aligned with the wisdom and power of God's eternal plan, and further secures the victory over the enemy.

SEVEN SCRIPTURAL ASPECTS OF THE APOSTOLIC CALL

How does the apostolic calling come to a person? Whether the call is to become an apostle, or simply an apostolic Christian, at least seven observations from the Scriptures solidify our understanding of the process.

1. *The apostolic call originates from deep within the Father's heart.* "Every good gift and every perfect gift is from above, and comes down from the Father of lights" (Jas. 1:17). The pre-incarnate Christ heard God's call first, and followed it to earth where He became flesh (see Heb. 10:5-7). There He echoed the call to chosen men. When Jesus explained "As the Father has sent Me, I also send you" (John 20:21), He used a specific word in the Greek for "send" and "sent." The word He chose was *apostello*, which is related to the word *apostolos*, from which we get the word "apostle." Christ, as an apostle, was the *sent one* of the Father, who now sends us in His behalf.

2. *The apostolic call, which comes from the Father, has its eternal residence in Christ, the Apostle* (see Gal. 1:1; Heb. 3:1). He is the heavenly Apostle who embodies and communicates everything an earthly apostle must be. Christ owns the apostolic ministry and is therefore the pattern Apostle. When Jesus called Peter and Andrew, it was on behalf of the Father, but He had the authority to call them. Jesus was an eternal reservoir of the apostolic calling the Father gave Him.

3. *Christ imparts His apostleship to people* (see Eph. 4:11). Peter and Andrew were ordinary people, but Jesus pursued them. Like a reservoir sharing its resources with surrounding waterways, Jesus deposit-

ed His call into them. When He was on earth, Jesus chose and trained apostles, exposing them to His own apostolic calling. As they received and obeyed the call, they reproduced themselves in others who continued the legacy. Thus the call that originated from the Father's heart and came through Christ to the first apostles has spanned the many generations between us and them. It is amazing that we are following Christ partly because they willingly yielded and became conduits of the call from the Father.

4. *The calling of an apostle is personal and specific.* Jesus told Peter and Andrew that He would make *them* fishers of men. Doubtless, other fishermen were present that day, but Jesus specifically chose them. As Christ transfers the Apostolic Spirit and call, He does it with purpose and precision; His virtue is not wasted. Not everyone is an apostle (see 1 Cor. 12:29). This calling, like every spiritual calling, comes as a personal subpoena from Christ. This fact becomes evident in the account of choosing Matthias to succeed Judas.

> And they prayed and said, "You, O Lord, who know the hearts of all, show which of these two You have chosen to take part in this ministry and apostleship from which Judas by transgression fell, that he might go to his own place." And they cast their lots, and the lot fell on Matthias. And he was numbered with the eleven apostles (Acts 1:24-26).

The apostles recognized that the choice had to be God's. No one can call himself as an apostle, but must be specifically called by Christ to stand in that office.

5. *The apostolic call is a command from God in Christ* (see 1 Tim. 1:1). Jesus did not ask Peter and Andrew to follow Him, He emphatically called them.

First Timothy 2:7 states that the call of an apostle is an ordination from God. The word translated "ordain" in this verse implies that certain people have been specifically made for this purpose, designed by God from before conception and brought forth to be an apostle. Nothing short of that purpose can be the basis of an apostolic calling.

6. *The apostolic call touches and transforms.* It carries the same transforming power that created the heavens and the earth from nothing. Christ does not call people because they possess apostolic character, but

chooses them and releases the apostolic calling upon them, which *changes* their characters. Peter and Andrew immediately left their nets and permanently changed the direction of their lives. Jesus called the twelve His "apostles" long before they were mature. Later, Peter's life would go through further radical changes, enabling Him to stand as a true father in the Church. This calling sets the apostolic person apart, separates that person to the gospel, and transforms who he or she is (see Rom. 1:1).

7. *The apostolic call results in the formation of an apostolic people.* The apostolic company increased exponentially as the apostles ministered. No wonder, for as we study Ephesians 4:7-16, we find that Christ has called apostles (along with prophets, evangelists, pastors and teachers) to contribute to the *increase* of the Body as equippers. The work of the apostle is clear: God desires that whatever the apostle possesses of the character and Spirit of Christ be imparted to the Body of Christ as it matures. If this were not so, God would never place an apostle as an equipper of the Body.

It is God's will that the entire Body of Christ become apostolic and reflect the fullness and image of Jesus the Apostle. That is not to imply that each person in the Body will become an apostle. Rather, God's design is that the apostle would spiritually affect the members of the Body of Christ and influence them to take on apostolic qualities.

To summarize, God the Father has given an apostolic calling to His Son, Jesus Christ. Christ has generously demonstrated and distributed the calling to specific individuals who become apostles. God then imparts an Apostolic Spirit and calling through these apostles to the entire Body of Christ as a reflection of His Spirit within them. This process is what we shall see increase in these last days as a part of the apostolic movement's influence. As the needs of a lost world touch the heart of the Father, the Son will gift more and more apostles, who will in turn perfect an apostolic people to reach the world. All of this rests on the clarity by which we perceive the eternal call as it is going forth to His people.

RESPONDING TO THE APOSTOLIC CALL

In many ways, the Church has been slow to walk in these truths, not properly understanding the full extent and reach of the apostolic call. From the preincarnate Christ through the first-century apostles through the generations, to our present day, the call is echoing. The apostles must come forth!

Why have we explained most of it away? Have we been idle, assuming that the apostolic calling was only temporary in the Church? Paul clearly says that apostles will function until the Body of Christ is fully matured (see Eph. 4:11-13). Others have maintained that even if apostles do exist, they are expected to bear the weight of all apostolic work. Their reasoning has been: Let the evangelists do the evangelizing. Let the apostles do the apostolic work. (More about the work of an apostle in chapter 7, "Planting and Watering for Increase"). Nothing could be further from the intention of the Father. No wonder real apostolic results have been scarce! It is as though we have obeyed a "Great Omission" instead of the Great Commission.

We must acknowledge that the entire Body of Christ is responsible for carrying out the apostolic vision of the Father at some level. None are excluded from the vineyard, though not all are apostles. "For many are called" (Matt. 20:16).

"AM I CALLED?"

One of the questions many will ask as they learn that God is calling forth apostles in this hour is: Am I one of them? Deep within each of us is a desire to be used effectively by God. The apostolic call is going forth, summoning some to become apostolic people, others to become apostles, and we must discern between the two. How does a person know if he or she is called beyond the role of an apostolic person to actually become an apostle?

The life of the apostle Paul becomes a picture of the apostle-level apostolic calling in action. Four progressive stages are involved in calling an apostle, and in the person's awareness of that calling:

1. The Intuition of a Call
The initial stage of a personal apostolic calling for Paul came to him intuitively. He knew that God was calling him as an apostle because God had shown it to him personally (see Gal. 1:15). For any apostle-in-the-making, the apostolic calling begins as an inner knowing or a spiritual sense that is clearly from God. This is just the beginning of a progressive outworking of the apostolic calling.

2. The Intimation of a Call

The next level of the personal calling Paul experienced came as an implication from Ananias just after Paul met Christ (see Acts 9:10-19). Jesus had told Ananias while he was in prayer that Paul was a chosen vessel. When Ananias prayed for Paul, he was filled with the Spirit. It is clear that Ananias shared his message from God with Paul, and though apostleship was not specifically mentioned, Paul's understanding that God was calling him was confirmed through another. Outside confirmation is an important key in the process of identifying and substantiating the apostolic call. Clearly Paul accepted the calling and began to pursue it from that day.

3. The Indication of a Call

As time went on, the intuition and intimation of the call progressed to a clear prophetic sanction. The best scriptural pattern we have for the process of selecting, ordaining and setting legitimate apostles into office is the account of the prophetic gathering at Antioch. As the apostles prayed at Antioch, Paul and Barnabas were singled out by the voice of God as chosen instruments (see Acts 13:2). This tells us that the appointment of apostles is a Spirit-led activity, that it is done publicly and in a context of prayer and worship, and that several proven leaders need to agree.

Make no mistake about it: To proceed in apostolic ministry without the keys of a prophetic, public and plural ordination by proven ministries would be entirely out of order in the emerging apostolic movement. Each candidate for the apostolic ministry must wait upon this kind of experience before pursuing the fullness of an apostolic call. In this way, many abuses and errors can be avoided. The apostolic network I am involved in uses this as the working pattern to guide us safely through the process of ordaining apostles.

We'll be discussing other safety factors for the apostolic movement throughout the book, but especially in chapter 8 where we'll examine the importance of proven character in apostles, and in chapter 11 where we'll look at the question of the checks and balances for apostolic authority.

4. The Impartation of a Call

The final confirmation of an apostolic calling came to Paul as hands were laid upon him in that same corporate gathering (see Acts 13:3). Upon hearing what the Spirit of God was saying, God used the brethren at Antioch to impart blessing and anointing to Paul and Barnabas. Laying on of hands imparted divine power into the lives of these apostles, and was the final seal upon their calling.

Each person God calls to participate in the emerging apostolic movement, whether called as an apostle or simply as an apostolic person, needs to discern the nature of a personal calling, and respond accordingly. The calling will come intuitively and will ultimately progress to an impartation of supernatural power.

Now it is necessary for us to be alert and responsive to the apostolic call. At Pentecost, a sound came from heaven with the outpouring (see Acts 2:2). Our ears must be open to the heavenly sound of our day. From beyond the realm of business as usual, to each of us Jesus says, "Follow Me." He is echoing the Father's heart. He is walking the shorelines of our lives, interrupting our activity and calling all of us to drop our nets in one dimension or another. When we do, we undergo radical changes; we become *apostolic people.*

CHANGING THE WORLD THROUGH APOSTOLIC PEOPLE

I REMEMBER READING A PAPERBACK BOOK MANY YEARS AGO WRITTEN BY Henk Vigeveno. The book was about Jesus and the twelve apostles and was entitled *Thirteen Men Who Changed the World* (Regal Books). I was so impressed by the concept that Jesus and just twelve followers had changed the world. I wanted to be a world changer too, but the title subtly reinforced a misconception in my mind; it seemed to confirm my fear that only a few significant people will be used by God to shape history. Unfortunately, as I read church history, I can see that I was not the only one in the Body of Christ who had that misconception. Many believe that only an elite few are used by God to change the world, but is that correct? Clearly the world needs changing, but who will do it?

THE CHURCH AS AN APOSTOLIC COMPANY

As the Body of Christ is restored to its New Testament pattern, God desires each member to be activated for His end-time plan to be fulfilled. That plan, as revealed in Ephesians 4, is that *every* member of the Body function in active ministry. That is how it was in the Early Church. Each believer was an active missionary. The Early Church did not depend solely upon professional leaders for its growth. Each Christian was both "priest" and "missionary."[1] Though we have failed to fully grasp this truth, things are beginning to change for the better. The world will be changed when the Church is transformed into a company of apostolic people.

The Church that witnesses the end of the age will be alive, victorious and activated in the gifts and callings of the Holy Spirit. The Body of Christ cannot be half asleep if we are to seize the opportunities of this hour. Can anything less than the entire Church moving in the power of the Spirit be sufficient to reap the final harvest of the nations?

The emerging company of apostles and apostolic people will be a world-changing force. Apostles will be sent into the world by the thousands as they hear and obey the apostolic call. It is inspiring to consider that this same call will go out to everyday people—those who are not apostles, but have the apostolic worldview and passion to be a part of the movement at various levels.

To assure that we are a part of this move, we must see that anyone who is sent by God is apostolic. The Scriptures confirm this. In the New Testament, the same language is used to describe the calling and activity of both apostles and apostolic people. Two closely related Greek words, apostolos (meaning apostle, or sent one) and apostello (meaning sent) lend great insight to our study. They are used to describe a group of people much larger than the twelve apostles; they are used to describe believers.

In the New Testament, an apostle is *one who is sent.* You do not have to be an apostle, however, to be described by the word *apostello.* You just have to be sent. That is quite significant, for when we view sending in this broader sense, we are able to understand that *many* are sent by the Lord.

This means that average men and women can be used by God in apostolic ways, totally apart from the office of an apostle. They may not be apostles, but they can be *apostolic.* The record of the early believers supports this.

> At that time a great persecution arose against the church which was at Jerusalem; and they were all scattered throughout the regions of Judea and Samaria, except the apostles. Therefore those who were scattered went everywhere preaching the word (Acts 8:1,4).

The members of the church at Jerusalem, not the apostles, were scattered abroad and spreading the gospel. This fact requires a broadening of the concept of apostolic ministry to one that includes the entire Body of Christ. God uses ordinary men and women in apostolic ways. History shows that the world is often changed by people of ordinary means who possess extraordinary virtues. Among those God uses in this way are a class of people—a new generation of Christians—that can be called apostolic people.

Together, apostles and these apostolic people comprise what can be called an apostolic company. Certainly the New Testament church was such a company—a great assembly of apostolic people under the direction of apostles, sent by the Holy Spirit to do apostolic work. In at least this instance, the apostles themselves stayed behind while the apostolic people went forth preaching under the guidance of the Holy Spirit.

The implications of this concept are enormous. What a marvelous pattern this provides for the Church today! In the emerging apostolic movement, we shall see a return to this framework. Thousands of apostles and multiplied thousands of apostolic people will form a worldwide apostolic company that will literally change the world as the Early Church did. We can no longer look to the pattern of just a few apostles doing apostolic works. We have a new and more biblical paradigm, one that acknowledges apostles and active apostolic people.

THE NEW TESTAMENT APOSTOLIC COMPANY

Keeping this paradigm in mind, consider the kinds of apostolic people we find in the New Testament. The use of the words *apostolos* and *apostello* reveal the entire spectrum of apostles and apostolic people to be found in Scripture. Together, these form the Body of the New Testament apostolic company to which we belong.

Jesus the Chief Apostle

"Therefore, holy brethren, partakers of the heavenly calling, consider the Apostle and High Priest of our confession, Christ Jesus" (Heb. 3:1). Jesus, who heads up the New Testament apostolic company, is the One sent by the Father to the world as an Apostle. He is the Savior of sinners and the Redeemer of fallen mankind. Christ is also the Prophet,

Teacher, Shepherd and Evangelist of the five ministries in Ephesians 4:11. As an Apostle, however, Christ remains the unique and eternal pattern for apostles to follow; He exhibits every quality the Father desires in an apostle.

The Twelve Apostles of the Lamb

Included in this company are the twelve apostles. "Then He appointed twelve, that they might be with Him and that He might send them out to preach, and to have power to heal sicknesses and to cast out demons" (Mark 3:14,15). Jesus chose the twelve apostles early in His earthly ministry. Christ conferred upon them the title of "apostle" (see Luke 6:13), and it is of interest that He never ordained people to any other office. The twelve apostles included Peter, James, John, Andrew, Philip, Nathaniel, Thomas, Matthew, James the son of Alphaeus, Simon, Thaddaeus and Judas who was replaced by Matthias. Christ shared His ministry with these twelve men.

The twelve are distinguished by several unique facts. Each of the twelve apostles of the Lamb personally witnessed the resurrection and ascension of Jesus (see Acts 1:9,22; 2:32; 3:15; 4:33; 5:30-32; 10:39-42). No one knew Christ more fully than they, and none have since been personally trained by Christ on earth. Because they worked and lived directly with Jesus, they shall remain preeminent among the entire apostolic company, and will possess a special prominence in the Kingdom that other New Testament apostles will not achieve (see Matt. 19:28; Rev. 21:14).

Other New Testament Apostles

It is clear that there were more apostles than the twelve apostles of the Lamb. These are referred to as secondary apostles by some theologians because they are designated in Scripture as apostles, but do not have the unique prominence in the Kingdom that the original twelve had. These apostles include some of the greatest world changers in history, and this kind of apostle continues on today as the normative kind.

The New Testament mentions the following names as those who were secondary apostles: Matthias (Acts 1:26); Paul (1 Cor. 15:8); James, the brother of Jesus (Gal. 1:19); Barnabas (Acts 14:3,4,14); Apollos (1 Cor. 4:6-9); Timothy (Acts 19:22; 1 Thess. 1:1; 2:6), Titus (2 Cor. 8:23, where "messenger" is *apostolos*); Silas or Silvanus (Acts 15:22; 1 Thess.

1:1; 2:6); Tychicus (2 Tim. 4:12); Judas (Acts 15:22; 1 Thess. 2:6); Andronicus (Rom. 16:7); Junia (whose name indicates this might have been a woman, Rom. 16:7—more about this in chapter 6); Epaphroditus (Phil. 2:25); Erastus (Acts 19:22); and two unnamed apostles (2 Cor. 8:23).

If the twelve apostles are added to this list, a total of 32 apostles would be mentioned in the New Testament. All of these were sent by God as valid apostolic ministers and members of the apostolic company of the New Testament.

The Seventy

"After these things the Lord appointed seventy others also, and sent them two and two before His face into every city and place where He Himself was about to go" (Luke 10:1). This broader Body of disciples was sent by Christ and went everywhere preaching and ministering healing and deliverance. The number 70 was special and symbolic in Israel. Seventy elders were present with Moses in the wilderness (see Num. 11:16-25) and they became symbolic of the Spirit of Christ coming on His people. Seventy was the "number" of the nations of the earth as found in Genesis 10. This number is a symbol of the whole earth to which the 70 were sent. Some writers maintain that the next generation of apostles was selected from among the 70 disciples.

The 70 disciples are included in our list of the apostolic company because they were the original apostolic people; that is, people who were sent and appointed by Christ for active ministry. Though they were not apostles, they did apostolic works—healing the sick, preaching the gospel, establishing the work of God—as apostolic people. This ties them to the Twelve and to the secondary apostles because they all operated under the same apostolic mandate from the hand of Christ.

All of Christ's Disciples

In a unique way, everyone who follows Christ as a disciple is part of the apostolic company. We are all the sent ones of the Lord: "As You sent [apostello] Me into the world, I also have sent [apostello] them into the world" (John 17:18). We are in Christ and partake of His anointing. The same unction that is in Christ and the apostles is upon us all: "Now he who establishes us with you in Christ and has anointed us is God" (2 Cor. 1:21). Because that anointing is upon us, we are apostolic people, even though not every one of us is called to be an apostle (see 1 Cor. 12:29).

This is the reasoning behind our definition of apostolic people as Christians who support and participate in apostolic ministry, but are not actual apostles.

AN APOSTOLIC COMPANY IS COMING FORTH!

A lot of responsibility comes with being counted among the apostolic company. In the book of Acts, the apostolic company of Christians was a mighty force of effective harvesters.

> Now those who were scattered after the persecution that arose over Stephen traveled as far as Phoenicia, Cyprus, and Antioch, preaching the word to no one but the Jews only. But some of them were men from Cyprus and Cyrene, who, when they had come to Antioch, spoke to the Hellenists, preaching the Lord Jesus. And the hand of the Lord was with them, and a great number believed and turned to the Lord (Acts 11:19-21).

God was with them, and multitudes turned to the Lord through their ministry. When the next great move of God hits the earth, we will see another company of apostolic people arising.

PROTOTYPICAL APOSTOLIC PEOPLE

The first five chapters of Acts focus largely on the church as a group, and what corporate life was like for them as a whole. Key leaders, such as Peter and John, figure prominently in these early pages. Beginning with chapter 6, certain people—ordinary in the sense that they were not prominent leaders—begin to be featured in Luke's narrative. Their lives typify the life of an apostolic person.

Consider Stephen, the amazing deacon. He was ordained to simply serve behind the scenes, doing natural tasks that would assist the apostles. Yet he was full of faith and power, working signs and wonders (see Acts 6:8). He preached the Word with such fire that he became the first Christian martyr. He was not an apostle, but he was definitely an apostolic person.

Another outstanding yet "ordinary" believer was Philip, the deacon (see 8:5ff). Philip was comfortable sharing his faith one on one, or preaching to large crowds. It seems clear despite the fact that he was not an apostle that signs, wonders and miracles were a frequent part of his ministry. Then there was Ananias, the brave helper of the newly converted apostle, Paul (see 9:10-19). Ananias was a man of prayer who heard the voice of God in great detail. Despite his understandable fear of Saul (as he was then known), Ananias obeyed the Spirit, prophesied to Paul, laid his hands on him and miraculously healed him. Ananias was not an apostle; he was just an ordinary believer whom God used in an extraordinary way.

Bill Scheidler alludes to the abundance of apostolic people in the New Testament when he says, "There seemed to be quite a number of people in the New Testament who did apostolic-type functions at times who were never specifically called apostles. Probably the best examples of these are the seventy that Christ sent out to do basically what the twelve had done in previous experiences. This seems to answer the question about many in our day who have been instrumental in some apostolic work but who do not appear to be specifically called to that life ministry. There are many in this category in the body of Christ."[2]

During the first decades of the Church, thousands of apostolic people could have been like Stephen and Philip and flowed with God supernaturally in their everyday lives. This is the kind of power God wants pervading His Church. To possess this power, we must carefully follow the pattern of these people, for we must understand and follow *apostolic principles* before we can hope to possess *apostolic power*.

OUTSTANDING FEATURES OF APOSTOLIC PEOPLE

What are the patterns of apostolic people? What will distinguish the emerging apostolic company as it arises? The New Testament richly describes the remarkable lives and activities of the Early Church, enabling us to draw upon those exciting days for the secrets to their power. Ten features are common for apostolic people. They are as follows:

1. Relational
One of the most amazing qualities of the people in the Early Church

was that they were in "one accord" (see 1:14; 2:1,46; 4:32; 5:12). Despite their varying racial, economic and cultural differences, they remained virtually unanimous in everything they did, from ministry to the Lord to ministry to each other. They did not allow their differences to divide them, which is a harmony that cannot be achieved by selfish people. Only those who make relationships with others a priority can access the resources required to live in harmony amid diversity.

The apostolic people of our generation will also be relational people. They will prioritize connecting with each other, including across racial, denominational and national boundaries. For a practical manifestation of this relational element in today's Church, see chapter 14, which describes apostolic networks.

2. Vibrant

The Early Church radiated an enthusiastic happiness and passion for what God was doing in its midst. The people were a glad people, full of vibrant joy as they received the Word, lived and ate together and preached the good news (see 2:41,46; 11:23; 13:48).

When God's Spirit comes upon His people, the fruit of joy is evident. The world eagerly awaits another people like this. As the Spirit is poured out upon us in these last days, we must become vibrant in all that we do for Him.

3. Reverent

Had the vibrancy of the early Christians made them casual or flippant about their faith, the Church would not have accomplished all it did. This was a people who possessed a sober awe and respect for God and His apostles. A holy "fear came upon every soul" (Acts 2:43; 5:5,11,13; see also 9:31).

What would happen if that same intense awareness of God's awesomeness came upon us today? It would move us, as it moved them, to take our faith—and the hour we live in—seriously. This same reverence and fear must be present in us as we live for God in this delicate point in history.

4. Focused

"They continued steadfastly" is a phrase that describes the early Christians' constant focus upon the Kingdom (2:42; see also 7:55; 14:9).

Despite the great excitement of the hour and the lack of organizational sophistication of the church, they were not distracted by the things that weigh down God's people today. Like an army, they had a singleness of vision and sense of mission to accomplish great things for God.

In what were they steadfast? They were diligent in keeping the apostles' doctrine, having fellowship, breaking bread and praying (see 2:42). They prioritized their activities around truths that would transform them, events that would gather them, covenant meals that would connect them and intercession that would empower them.

If we are to be an apostolic people, this kind of focus must be found in us, for we are commanded, "Be steadfast, immovable, always abounding in the work of the Lord, knowing that your labor is not in vain in the Lord" (1 Cor. 15:58).

5. Unselfish

Consider the ability of the Early Church to take care of the needy (see 2:44; 4:32-35). What must their attitudes have been to generate this kind of commitment to one another? They were an unselfish people, willing to share what was theirs with those who lacked, free from the kind of selfishness that keeps people focused only on themselves. They sensitively shared their resources and demonstrated the great virtue of love. In doing so, they became a true pattern for us.

6. Positive

Acts 2:47 says they were "praising God," a simple clue to their joyful optimism. Not a people of worry, fear or pessimism; they were aware that they had a great God and an exciting destiny. They enthusiastically gave glory to the Lord, even in the worst circumstances. It was one of their greatest qualities.

The challenge that lies ahead for the emerging generation of apostolic people will require that we aerate our spirits with this same positive attitude generated through wholehearted praise to God. Without it, we cannot be truly apostolic.

7. Attractive

The believers in the Early Church were magnetic people. Just as Jesus had, they won the favor of the general public (see Luke 2:52; Acts 2:42). They were winsome and admired by society. They never allowed the gospel message to become bad news; it remained good news—an attractive message—in their presentation to the people. Only the religious hated them.

What would happen if the Church today gained this same quality? People would be powerfully drawn to the Christ in us, instead of feeling that we are, by and large, irrelevant to their lives.

8. Anointed

These men and women were full of the dynamic life of the Holy Spirit (see Acts 2:4; 4:8,31; 6:3,5; 7:55; 9:17; 11:24; 13:52). The believers depicted in Acts were filled with God's Spirit through times of prayer and waiting on Him. Spiritual visitation was the center of their activity. They understood and experienced times of refreshing (see 3:19), and walked with a radiant grace upon their lives (see 4:33).

Without this same anointing present in us, we can never hope to be anything resembling an apostolic people. We must rediscover the place of prayer in the Church, so that we can walk as these believers walked, radiating the life of God wherever we go.

9. Bold

Though speaking in tongues has been emphasized as the initial evidence of the infilling of the Spirit by many, we may have overlooked the fact that a more prominent manifestation of that experience in Scripture is bold preaching of the Word (see 4:13, 29,31; 9:27,29; 13:46; 14:3; 18:26; 19:8; 28:31). These believers were outspoken, unreserved and clear in communicating with the world.

The quality of boldness is just as essential today for the apostolic proclamation of truth, and is a major indication of a right relationship with God: "The wicked flee when no one pursues, but the righteous are bold as a lion" (Prov. 28:1).

10. Progressive

A striking reality of the Early Church is that it quickly broke with the standard religious conventions of the day. For example, the Temple was the center of activity for Jewish people, and yet the disciples quickly adapted to the use of homes as meeting places. This shift showed an openness in the Christian community to new ways of doing things. Creative thinking was allowed to guide their activity. They were free from the prevailing religious methods, and as a result, the Church was effective and grew at an astonishing rate.

The Church today is beginning to show these same signs of innovation and practical thinking. Fresh, God-directed methods of outreach, education and discipleship, and inspiring approaches to worship services and ministry to one another will breathe life into our activities. These can be the new wineskins that help us contain the new wine God is pouring into us so that we may joyfully face the challenges of this new day.

BECOMING AN APOSTOLIC PEOPLE

When we calculate the enormous task of world evangelization that has become the responsibility of this generation, we must depend upon a sweeping move of the Holy Spirit as the greatest factor for success. More than 2 billion remain unacquainted with the true saving power of Christ. We have used satellites, video and shortwave radio to reach them. Although progress has been made, it is only by becoming more apostolic that we hope to see the world turned upside down for Him.

As the apostolic company emerges, it will demonstrate these outstanding traits we find in the Early Church. The new generation of apostolic believers will be a relational, vibrant, reverent, focused, unselfish, positive, attractive, anointed, bold and progressive company of men and women who help take the world by storm. Can anything short of that produce a successful harvest? As Peter Wagner puts it, "We need a continually growing army of men and women who have whatever spiritual gift or gifts are necessary to reach billions of unreached peoples in our generation."[3]

God will not call just 12 apostles to change the world. Instead, He will establish a vast company of apostles and everyday apostolic people who will be supernaturally empowered. The Holy Spirit will be poured out upon the entire Church in a brand new dimension, and then it will be able to accomplish its mission.

Our purpose as a people is to become like Christ, the great Apostle. This will be accomplished in part as a result of an apostolic movement. When we move in this apostolic anointing and manifest the qualities of apostolic people, it will not mean that we are apostles; it will mean that we are Christians.

Notes

1. Tim Dowley, John H. Y. Briggs, Robert D. Londer, David F. Wright, eds. *Eerdman's Handbook to the History of Christianity* (Grand Rapids: Eerdman's, 1977), p. 70.
2. Bill Scheidler, *The New Testament Church and Its Ministries* (Portland, Oreg.: Bible Temple, 1980), p. 89.
3. C. Peter Wagner, *Your Spiritual Gifts Can Help Your Church Grow* (Ventura, Calif.: Regal, 1979; revised edition, 1994), p. 186.

THE APOSTOLIC SPIRIT

WHEN PRESIDENT REAGAN WAS SHOT IN 1981, THE NATION'S HEART SKIPPED a beat. It was so unexpected that a wave of shock was felt from coast to coast and around the world. At first, it was unclear how seriously he was wounded. Immediately a double guard was posted by Vice President Bush, who was away from Washington at the time. Various wheels of government turned, preparing to confer presidential powers upon him should the president be unable to function.

The fear that Reagan would die gradually gave way to reports that his recovery was expected. The nation learned that the president would not have survived had the bullet been positioned differently by just one inch. As if by providence, his life was spared. The world heaved a collective sigh of relief.

Amid the confusion, however, then Secretary of State Alexander Haig made a serious blunder. In an attempt to calm the nation in the early moments after this shocking news hit, he declared to the national media that he was "in charge." His statement was erroneous, because Vice President Bush was next in order of succession, followed by the speaker of the House. Haig was forced to later correct himself, much to his own chagrin.

Haig's error was fueled by a momentary misunderstanding of the process of the delegation of powers between a head of state and his successors. The president, vice president, speaker of the House and secretary of state play specific roles in our nation's power structure.

This line of authority descends from the top level down to various levels, including members of the cabinet, various envoys and official ambassadors. If any one of these function apart from clear boundaries, blunders such as Haig's may result. Confusion, embarrassment and even danger are always near when roles are misunderstood in any authority structure.

Apostles have a unique and dependent relationship with the Holy Spirit. In much the same way that a head of state shares powers with appointed officers, God Almighty, the head of state in the kingdom of God, shares His power with the apostles (as well as prophets, evangelists, pastors and teachers) through the Holy Spirit. When a head of state sends an ambassador as a representative, we may be reminded of the Holy Spirit's relationship to the apostle. Apostles may most clearly be understood in terms of their roles as *ambassadors from heaven*. They are sent by the Holy Spirit as emissaries of the King bearing a message from the throne of God.

THE HOLY SPIRIT IS APOSTOLIC

As we have already observed, the Spirit of God is an Apostolic Spirit. Keeping in mind all of the other wonderful attributes that the Holy Spirit has, we must not overlook this key aspect. Why do we call the Holy Spirit an Apostolic Spirit? Because his makeup and identity are apostolic, and His work is apostolic. Indeed, the entire apostolic movement will be permeated with the presence, power and activity of the Holy Spirit. Consider these four facts about the Holy Spirit:

1. *The Holy Spirit has been sent* (see John 14:26; 16:7,8; Acts 2:4; Gal. 4:6). Jesus spoke of both Himself and the Father as sending the Holy Spirit to teach, empower, guide and comfort His people. Like a heavenly apostle, He has been sent from heaven on a mission to the world to "convict the world of sin, and of righteousness, and of judgment" (John 16:8).

2. *The Holy Spirit sends.* He is the One who sent the gospel "from heaven" (1 Pet. 1:12). He also sends the messengers who carry the message in the form of prophets and other people of God (see Isa. 48:16). Jesus Himself recognized that He came as One sent: "The Spirit of the Lord God is upon Me,...He has sent Me to heal the brokenhearted" (Isa. 61:1). You will remember that the essence of apostleship involves *being*

sent. Thus, if the Holy Spirit has been sent and He Himself sends, He is apostolic.

3. *The Holy Spirit initiates apostolic activity*. When the Holy Spirit was sent on the Day of Pentecost, the result was an activation of true apostolic ministry. From that Upper Room came apostles and apostolic people that changed the world. These previously ordinary men and women were transformed into an apostolic company because the Apostolic Spirit came upon them. This tells us that the Spirit who generated these results must Himself be apostolic.

4. *The Holy Spirit is apostolic because He is a member of the Godhead.* The whole Trinity is permeated with the Apostolic Spirit. Jesus Christ, the great Apostle (see Heb. 3:1), demonstrated the Apostolic Spirit when He sent forth the apostles to do apostolic work (see Matt. 10:5; Mark 3:14). As an Apostle Himself, He conceived the human apostolic office and gave it to the Church (see Eph. 4:11). The Father also reflected the Apostolic Spirit when He sent Jesus into the world on the greatest apostolic mission ever (see Matt. 10:40; John 7:29; 17:18). Jesus indicated that the Father is responsible to hear our prayers and send forth workers to reap the harvest (see Matt. 9:38). All of heaven blends together in a symphony of apostolic activity to affect the world with the love of God.

THE HOLY SPIRIT'S RELATIONSHIP WITH APOSTLES

What is the function of the Holy Spirit in the ministry of the apostle? The Spirit of God assumes at least five roles in His oversight of the apostle of Christ:

1. The Apostle's Separator

When the people at Antioch gathered together to minister to the Lord, the Spirit's voice was heard. "As they ministered to the Lord and fasted, the Holy Spirit said, 'Now *separate* to Me Barnabas and Saul for the work to which I have called them'" (Acts 13:2, emphasis mine). Paul later wrote to the church at Rome in reference to that moment that he had been "called to be an apostle, *separated* to the gospel of God" (Rom. 1:1, emphasis mine).

To separate in this case literally means to *set off by a boundary*. The idea is to draw clear boundary lines to establish a definite territory within which the apostle is meant to operate with full authority. The apostle has a spiritual dominion and territory delineated by God. We are reminded that we should not cross the boundary lines that surround apostleship, or go too far with ambitious intrusion into any ministry to which we are not called. It also means to appoint to an office or position of authority, just as an ambassador is appointed by a head of state.

Being separated as an apostle is something much higher than an appointed ambassador. It denotes being sanctified, approved and enabled for divine service. As with the Old Testament Nazirite, who was separated from birth to serve the Lord, God makes the apostle holy and set apart for divine service:

> "Speak to the children of Israel, and say to them: 'When either a man or woman consecrates an offering to take the vow of a Nazirite, to *separate* himself to the Lord, he shall *separate* himself from wine and similar drink; he shall drink neither vinegar made from wine nor vinegar made from similar drink; neither shall he drink any grape juice, nor eat fresh grapes or raisins. All the days of his *separation* he shall eat nothing that is produced by the grapevine, from seed to skin. All the days of the vow of his *separation* no razor shall come upon his head; until the days are fulfilled for which he *separated* himself to the Lord, he shall be holy. Then he shall let the locks of the hair of his head grow. All the days that he *separates* himself to the Lord he shall not go near a dead body. He shall not make himself unclean even for his father or his mother, for his brother or his sister, when they die, because his *separation* to God is on his head. All the days of his *separation* he shall be holy to the Lord'" (Num. 6:2-8, emphasis mine).

Both Paul and John spoke of apostles as possessing this kind of separation. Ephesians 3:5 says, "Which in other ages was not made known to the sons of men, as it has been revealed by the Spirit to His *holy apostles* and prophets" (see also Rev. 18:20, emphasis mine). Being an apostle requires a life of practical holiness and separation.

The separation of a life for apostleship is an awesome experience made real to individuals by the Holy Spirit. It is a definite experience. Paul never doubted that he had been separated and appointed by the Holy Spirit. Though others questioned his authority, Paul clearly understood that he was chosen and called as an apostle. No human had given him this spiritual calling (see Rom. 13:1).

In the spiritual sense, people cannot ordain apostles as such, but can only *recognize* the separation of individuals by the Holy Spirit. In this process, apostles are unshakably aware of their calling through the Holy Spirit, and those who are sensitive to the Spirit will inevitably have their calling confirmed as at Antioch (see Acts 13:1-3). Later on we will explore the ordination process of apostles. For now, we should simply keep in mind that this activity is directed by the Spirit.

2. The Apostle's Sender

Just as heads of state have occasions to send ambassadors to other domains to perform business, so the Holy Spirit sends the apostle to humankind to do business for the King of kings. When the prophets and teachers at Antioch laid their hands on Barnabas and Saul, the Bible says they were "sent out by the Holy Spirit" (Acts 13:4). The apostle thus functions as a representative sent from God. This is consistent with the definition of an apostle as being "one sent."

Sending implies valid ordination and authorization. It is heaven's certification on a person's life. The ultimate authentication of any ministry has to do with whether or not the person has been sent by God (see Jer. 14:14,15; 28:9). A person cannot claim apostleship unless that person has been sent by the Holy Spirit.

The Holy Spirit sent the Lord Jesus as the great Apostle to earth to conduct the business of redemption and reconciliation on behalf of the Father. It was the greatest apostolic journey of all time. For this, Jesus was anointed, empowered and sent:

> "The *Spirit of the Lord* is upon Me, because He has anointed Me to preach the gospel to the poor; *He has sent Me* to heal the brokenhearted, to proclaim liberty to the captives and recovery of sight to the blind, to set at liberty those who are oppressed" (Luke 4:18, emphasis mine).

The Spirit of the Lord anointed and sent Jesus. His anointing preceded His sending, and His miraculous ministry resulted from His anointing. His wonderful work included healing broken hearts, preaching, delivering captives, restoring sight for the blind and liberating the bruised. These marvelous gestures of love on behalf of the Father point to the ministry Christ's apostles should manifest as they partake of the same calling and anointing.

Jesus had an intense awareness of the fact that He was sent:

But he answered and said, "I was not *sent* except to the lost sheep of the house of Israel" (Matt. 15:24, emphasis mine).

But he said to them, "I must preach the kingdom of God to other cities also, because for *this purpose I have been sent* (Luke 4:43, emphasis mine).

As Jesus was sent by the Father, so He sends His apostles to the nations on official kingdom business: "So Jesus said to them again, 'Peace to you! *As the Father has sent Me, I also send you'*" (John 20:21, emphasis mine).

As previously mentioned, the New Testament word *apostolos* means "sent one." Jesus is the sent one of the Father, and apostles are the sent ones of Christ. Just as He was empowered, anointed and sent by the Holy Spirit, Christ Himself empowers, anoints and sends His apostles to extend His ministry of apostleship around the world.

A word of caution is appropriate at this point. Ted Haggard, an internationally respected pastor and author, recently told me of a man who went crazy with this truth. A total stranger came to him after a service and proclaimed himself to be "sent by the Holy Spirit" as the new apostle over pastor Ted and the New Life Church! As you can imagine, this man's presumptive and demanding claim was instantly rejected as bogus. The incident was amusing because it was so far out, and yet it was disturbing because it typifies the imbalance of all too many who profess an apostolic calling today.

Being sent by the Holy Spirit as an apostle requires the fulfillment of the whole panorama of scriptural qualifications of apostolic ministry, not the least of which is humility. A servant's spirit is incompatible with pushy demands for position and unilateral submission. We hope such antics will be held to a minimum in the emerging apostolic movement. (We'll share more ideas about balancing authority and true ministry in chapters 10 and 11.)

3. The Apostle's Source

No ambassador goes forth in personal power. Instead, the ambassador is given authority from a higher power. The same is true of the apostle, whose base of power and authority is found in the Spirit. We'll be looking in greater detail at both power and authority as they relate to apostles in chapters 11 and 12.

The Spirit of God is seen in Scripture as being a source of awesome power. Micah declared he was "full of *power by the Spirit of the Lord*" (Mic. 3:8, emphasis mine). Mary conceived the Son of God by the power of the Spirit (see Luke 1:38). After fasting and overcoming Satan's temptations, Jesus emerged from the wilderness in the *"power of the Spirit"* to inaugurate His miracle ministry (Luke 4:14). The great apostle Jesus was able to manifest the fullness of His ministry because He was anointed "with the *Holy Spirit and with power*" and "went about doing good and healing all who were oppressed by the devil, for God was with Him" (Acts 10:38, emphasis mine).

In the same way, power for apostolic ministry comes from the Holy Spirit. The promise came to the apostles and those who were with them: "But you shall receive power when the Holy Spirit has come upon you; and you shall be witnesses to Me in Jerusalem, and in all Judea and Samaria, and to the end of the earth" (Acts 1:8). Full apostleship came for the Twelve at Pentecost under the influence of God's Spirit. Without such power, the apostles would have been totally helpless; with it, they became instruments for God to touch the world with His love and power.

4. The Apostle's Supervisor

In the book of Acts it is fascinating to read of the constant supervision the Holy Spirit exercised over the apostles. The apostles were men of great understanding and compassion, to be sure, but the Holy Spirit left them with more for direction than their own natural impulses. The Holy Spirit continually and specifically guided them in their efforts. Wiser than any earthly head of state, the Spirit bade them to go. What king would send forth an ambassador without specific directions and objectives at every point of the way?

An example of the Holy Spirit's constant watch care over the apostles is found in Acts 16:6-10 (emphasis mine):

> Now when they had gone through Phrygia and the region of Galatia, they were *forbidden by the Holy Spirit* to preach the word in Asia. After they had come to Mysia, they tried to go into Bithynia, but *the Spirit did not permit them.* So passing by Mysia, they came down to Troas. And a vision appeared to Paul in the night. A man of Macedonia stood and pleaded with him, saying, "Come over to Macedonia and help us." Now after he had seen the vision, immediately we sought to go to Macedonia, concluding that *the Lord had called us* to preach the gospel to them.

Like a masterful supervisor, the Spirit of God literally directed every leg of their journeys. The apostles made certain plans and at times their Supervisor said no. Other directions came and they obeyed those and had success.

The Holy Spirit's guidance frequently came through impressions, dreams, visions and prophecies. From this particular divine redirection came the successful foundations for the great church that was later raised up at Philippi, and our beloved New Testament book of Philippians.

Clearly the apostles understood the value of the Holy Spirit's supervision as they went forth. They sought His influence on their decisions every step of the way. This required true humility and spiritual sensitivity combined with a willingness to let go of all other natural plans. The result of this yieldedness was that they enjoyed unprecedented success.

What results would occur in modern missions if this same desire for divine supervision were more a part of our ministries? If more ministries today were receptive to this kind of guidance and supervision, we would certainly have gained more territory for the Lord by this time.

5. The Apostle's Seal

When ambassadors carried messages on behalf of kings, the letters would normally be sealed with the king's seal (see Gen. 41:42; 1 Kings 21:8; Esther 8:8). This was often applied from an impression in wax of the king's own ring, called a signet. This served to authenticate the correspondence that was often extremely sensitive. Upon opening the letter, the recipient would see the seal and be assured of the validity of its contents.

In much the same way, the Spirit of God acts as a seal upon the message of an apostle. In fact, Scripture is emphatic that the Spirit of God seals all of His people:

> Who also has sealed us and given us the Spirit in our hearts as a guarantee (2 Cor. 1:22).

> In Him you also trusted, after you heard the word of truth, the gospel of your salvation; in whom also, having believed, you were sealed with the Holy Spirit of promise (Eph. 1:13).

> And do not grieve the Holy Spirit of God, by whom you were sealed for the day of redemption (Eph. 4:30).

What is the manifestation of the seal of the apostle? It involves the image of two of the greatest works the Spirit of God ever performs. First, the seal is marked by changed lives. When Paul defended his apostleship, he argued powerfully with the Corinthians: "If I am not an apostle to others, yet doubtless I am to you. For you are the seal of my apostleship in the Lord" (1 Cor. 9:2). An apostle is certified by the evidence of a changed life.

Second, the work of the Holy Spirit becomes a seal on the apostle as evidenced through supernatural signs, wonders and mighty deeds: "Truly the signs of an apostle were accomplished among you with all perseverance, in signs and wonders and mighty deeds" (2 Cor. 12:12). To Paul, such signs were valuable in validating the ministry of a true apostle, and for that reason, we need to consider whether or not an increase in this kind of ministry is desirable for today. I believe it is, though it certainly is not as important as proven character in apostolic ministry (see chapter 8 "The Signs of an Apostle," where I deal directly with this question).

I'm convinced that many people in ministry today are apostles, although they do not regularly experience the kind of signs, wonders and miracles to which Paul is referring. Ultimately, I believe we will need to reckon with the message of this verse as the fullness of the apostolic ministry comes forth on the earth. The fact remains that changed lives and miraculous manifestations of God's power are a part of King Jesus' signet seal on the authentic ambassador from heaven and the important message that ambassador delivers.

Understanding the role of the apostle within the kingdom of God apart from his relationship to the Holy Spirit is impossible. Though politicians may be briefly confused about lines of power in a national emergency, the Body of Christ cannot afford to be confused about the apostles' line of power, especially in the critical hour in which we live. Apostles are inseparably bound to the Holy Spirit and depend completely on Him as their separator, sender, source, supervisor and sealer.

6

WHAT IS AN APOSTLE?

LIKE MOST BUSY PEOPLE TODAY, I HAVE HAD MANY OCCASIONS TO TRAVEL ON airplanes. I find many aspects of flight fascinating, but one of the greatest moments in air travel occurs when the skies are cloudy. During its demanding ascent, the plane will usually become slowly coated with moisture until it is suddenly engulfed in the foggy mists of the clouds. Visibility is instantly reduced to zero, and for a moment, the disorientation can be slightly unsettling. Then, as suddenly as the plane entered the fog, it emerges from it. A sense of relief and awe erupt within me as the plane swiftly breaks through the grayness into a brilliant panorama of crystal-clear skies above. The visibility that had been so limited swiftly becomes almost infinite. This thrilling moment offers a powerful analogy.

A FOGGY UNDERSTANDING

As we consider the apostle's definition, it is apparent that we must rise above an intellectual and spiritual fog if we are to come into crystal-clear understanding. Few ministries have posed the difficulty in being defined and accepted today as that of the apostle. Not many understand or appreciate this role in the Church. As Vinson Synan has noted, "Most people in church history who have claimed to be new apostles have been branded as heretics and excommunicated from the church."[1] Do God's people avoid understanding the apostle's ministry as though this information were somehow taboo? The purpose of this chapter—and this book—is to help lift the fog that keeps us in darkness.

As an example of our tendency to evade the subject, consider our approach to the word "apostle" itself. Many in the Church today would shudder to hear someone refer to a believer as an apostle, though we have no such problem with other ministry titles such as pastor and evangelist.

Wayne Grudem, a theologian, suggests: "If any in modern times want to take the title of 'apostle' to themselves, they immediately raise the suspicion that they may be motivated by inappropriate pride and desires for self-exaltation, along with excessive ambition and a desire for much more authority in the Church than any one person should rightfully have."[2] To escape the discomfort of the actual term "apostle," have we arbitrarily retired it and replaced it with the more sanitary title of "missionary" (a term not found in Scripture)?

It is hard to understand why we are so inconsistent. We universally understand and accept the roles of pastors and teachers within the Body of Christ, and we cannot imagine how the Church could function without them. The evangelist's ministry has become conspicuous in the Church during the past 100 years after centuries of invisibility, and we can easily recognize the indispensable role in the growth of the Church that evangelists have played. And within the past decade or so, even the mysterious ministry of the New Testament prophet has been examined, amplified and largely accepted in the Church. Why then has it been so hard for us to clarify the subject of apostleship and to see it exercised and implemented with scriptural success?

This state of affairs in the Church has occurred for several potential reasons. Certainly God cannot be responsible for any confusion relative to this subject, for 1 Corinthians 14:33 states: "God is not the author of confusion but of peace."

In natural terms, people may, out of a sense of humility, tend to avoid considering the subject because the office is perceived as lofty. Or perhaps because the idea that apostles are for today has been traditionally rejected, we have not seen the need for intensively evaluating this ministry. Cessationist theologians have long asserted that the office of apostle died at the close of the first century, and have persuaded the Body of Christ to scrap this ministry and its viability for today. Equally to blame may be the scant demonstration of this ministry through church history, even among those who profess faith in its existence.

AN EVIL INFLUENCE

At least one spiritual reason exists for the lack of understanding in the area of apostles. Satan, the great deceiver, is at the heart of all darkness and ignorance, and his attempts to cloud the issue have been deliberate. The apostle may well represent the single greatest human threat in existence to the work of Satan.

Wherever apostolic ministry functions, a spirit of confusion seems to arise and attempts to neutralize it. In Acts 17, after Paul's ministry in a Thessalonican synagogue had begun to produce converts, "But the Jews which believed not, moved with envy, took unto them certain lewd fellows of the baser sort, and gathered a company, and set all the city on an *uproar*, and assaulted the house of Jason, and sought to bring them out to the people." (v. 5, *KJV*, emphasis mine). In Acts 19, after the apostolic ministry of Paul had produced miracles, deliverances and conversions in Ephesus, "the whole city was filled with *confusion*" (v. 29, emphasis mine). It is no accident that in our day the fog of confusion has engulfed the Body of Christ in regard to apostles. The enemy will use whatever means he can to prevent the Body of Christ from recognizing the office of the apostle.

How the enemy dreads the apostle! How he fears the full restoration of this ministry! A New Testament apostolic function fully deployed within the Church today would significantly impact the dominion of darkness. Satan knows this, and I'm sure all of hell shudders at the prospect of a revitalization of apostles and apostolic people. Satan's clear objective is to create confusion regarding the subject and to cloud our understanding.

FOUNDATIONS FOR
UNDERSTANDING THE APOSTLE

Several truths are essential in understanding the role of the apostle. We need to consider these as foundational to clarity and build our knowledge upon them. Then, throughout the next several chapters, we will be able to elaborate in further detail.

Duration of the Apostle

The first question we must answer is, *Are apostles for today?* One devastating deception of the enemy against advancing the Church has been propagating a misconception that says Apostles were not intended to operate beyond the first century.

Some Christians assume the ministry of apostles ceased along with the New Testament era. They fail to *differentiate between the original apostolic function represented in "the Twelve" and the perennial apostolic function.* The result is the Church is denied the benefits of an apostolic ministry today.[3]

> Complex intellectual arguments have been erected against the validity of modern apostles despite the clear teaching of Scripture. Reflecting this position, Dr. Lewis Sperry Chafer wrote: "The service of those designated here (in Ephesians 4:11) as apostles evidently ceased with the first generation of the Church, *for no such qualified ministry is to be recognized in the Church today"* (Chafer, 1948; 217).[4]

> Others contend the functional role of the apostle has always remained in the Church. Alan R. Tippett writes: The word *apostle* is not confined to the Twelve. Barnabas, for example, was called an apostle (Acts 14:14), having been called and sent (Acts 13:2-3). Here the sender is the Holy Spirit acting through the Church. It would seem from such references as Rom. 16:7 and Eph. 4:11 that God *intended the functional role of apostleship to continue in the Church* (Tippett, 1969; 44-45).[5]

The question of the perennial function of apostles can only be answered by examining the Bible. It is evident that the twelve apostles hold a unique and authoritative position in the Kingdom. The existence of apostles beyond the number of the twelve in the New Testament is equally clear. Paul was one of them and, as we have already seen, Scripture provides a list of others who are called apostles (for a listing of their names, see my section "Other New Testament Apostles" in chapter 4). The confusion between the twelve apostles (who are unique and whose function is complete) and the other apostles in the New Testament (whose function is assumed by some to be complete, but is not) has fueled the error of believing that the office has ceased.

Peter Wagner finds, "The biblical evidence strongly supports the continuity of the gift of apostle. The original twelve apostles have a unique place in Christian history and they will be commemorated permanently in the New Jerusalem (see Rev. 21:14), but they were not the only apostles. First Corinthians 15 mentions that after the resurrection Jesus appeared to 'the twelve' and then also to 'all the apostles,' indicating that there were apostles other than the twelve (see 1 Cor. 15:5, 7). Furthermore, the warnings against 'false apostles' would be nonsense if apostles were limited to the twelve (see 2 Cor. 11:13; Rev. 2:2)."[6] He also notes, "Through the ages as well as today, many of God's gifted servants have been and are true apostles."[7]

Three additional compelling reasons for the existence of apostles today must be considered:

1. *We need them.* It is hard to imagine how the Church can expand and influence the world apart from Spirit-empowered people who can match the work of the first apostolic movement. Apostles are greatly needed by the Church today.

2. *Scripture never indicates that the office of the apostle would cease.* They are not viewed in Scripture as spiritual dinosaurs who were meant to become extinct in some kind of preordained ice age. Not a single verse can be reasonably construed to suggest that apostles were temporary.

3. *The Bible teaches that they will function perennially.* This is, of course, the most compelling argument for validating a present-day apostolic function. Paul states that apostles (as well as prophets, evangelists, pastors and teachers) will continue to perform in the plan of God until "we all come to the unity of the faith and of the knowledge of the Son of God, to a perfect man, to the measure of the stature of the fullness of Christ" (Eph. 4:13). That word "until" is important. Clearly the Church has not yet arrived at that place of perfection and maturity. The apostle must remain an enduring function, office and call as an essential part of the Body of Christ until that objective is accomplished.

Distinctions of the Apostle
We cannot fully understand the Church as an organism or as a Body until we understand the position of the apostle in the membership of

the Body. Although each member in the Body is indispensable, the apostle remains one of the most essential and primary members in the corporate Body of Christ.

The apostle is distinct from the other ministry gifts mentioned in Scripture and appears to possess a unique place, function and importance in God's plan. Apostles are considered God's first appointment in the membership of the body:

> And God has appointed these in the church: first apostles, second prophets, third teachers, after that miracles, then gifts of healings, helps, administrations, varieties of tongues. Are all apostles? Are all prophets? Are all teachers? Are all workers of miracles? Do all have gifts of healings? Do all speak with tongues? Do all interpret? (1 Cor. 12:28-30).

> And He Himself gave some to be apostles, some prophets, some evangelists, and some pastors and teachers (Eph. 4:11).

We cannot fully understand the Church as the temple of the living God until we properly assess the apostle as a foundational ministry (see Rom. 16:20; 1 Cor. 3:9-16; 9:1). A foundation in any structure is indispensable; it provides strength, stability and is the key to expansion potential. This quality of the apostolic ministry is also apparent in Scripture:

> According to the grace of God which was given to me, as a wise master builder I have laid the foundation, and another builds on it. But let each one take heed how he builds on it (1 Cor. 3:10).

> Having been built on the foundation of the apostles and prophets, Jesus Christ Himself being the chief cornerstone (Eph. 2:20).

As a foundational ministry, the apostle serves together with the prophet to lay the foundation for the entire temple of God, while receiving alignment and positioning from the cornerstone, Jesus Christ. Without the apostle as a member of the ongoing foundation of the Church, we cannot fully become the temple of the living God. The apostle cannot be omitted as a primary member of the Body of Christ, or as a foundational structure of the temple of God.

Dimensions of the Apostle

Apostles are not only to be viewed in terms of their duration and distinction, but their dimension must also be considered. That is, apostles must be understood and appreciated for what they are, but in this process care must be taken to avoid attributing more to them than does the Word of God.

Two mistaken mind-sets exist about apostleship within the Body of Christ that need to change. One involves underappreciating the ministry of an apostle (as we have seen), and the other involves attributing *more* to the apostle than is legitimate. The Body of Christ at times seems to deify apostles when we are not denying their existence.

An example of this sort of overappreciation of leaders is seen in the life of William Branham, a pioneer in the post-World War II healing revivals. Although some believe he had a legitimate ministry at first, he appears to have become deluded near the end of his life and was deified by himself and those around him. He proclaimed himself to be the angel of Revelation 3:14 and 10:7. After his death, some of his followers expected him to be resurrected and still others believed he was God and was virgin born.[8]

In measuring the dimensions of the apostolic office, we must be careful not to exaggerate the apostle's place of importance to the point of imbalance. Although apostles are primary in the Body of Christ, they are only human and as such they will be imperfect and fallible. Certainly neither apostolic people nor the apostolic movement will be perfect. Each apostolic person and each apostle represents only a fraction of the total equation. The Body is composed of many members, and it takes all of them working together to accomplish the will of God.

Development of the Apostle

Another important foundation to consider in the quest to understand the ministry of apostles involves their spiritual development. Again, because of the tendency to almost deify apostles, some may make the mistake of not allowing them room for growth and development. Apostles mature gradually as do those with any other ministry gift.

The term "apostle" has traditionally provoked an image of a fully seasoned person, overflowing with wisdom and experience. This may leave some with the impression that only the most mature can be called to this position.

Nothing could be further from the truth. In the case of the Twelve, Christ referred to them as apostles when they were still immature and unproven (see Luke 6:12). Peter is an excellent example of a man who began his apostleship full of instability and irrationality, but grew into marvelous maturity. He was in a process, not always mature, but always an apostle nevertheless.

The Lord builds upon the potential of a person. A believer may be called to be an apostle while still immature. Apostles can be people in progress—people under construction—while the seed of apostleship is present deep in their spirits. Jesus Christ creates apostles and calls them as apostles long before many would recognize them as such. Bill Scheidler insightfully points to a detailed process in developing an apostle, based on his study. The reader may find this helpful.[9]

Diversities of Apostles

Finally, it is important to consider the limitless diversity that must exist within the apostolic office. Apostles are a diverse group, and no single apostle sets a pattern for apostleship, unless we consider Jesus Christ. An infinite variety of forms and functions are present in the gift of apostleship. None of the apostles in the New Testament ministered in precisely the same way. Just as a variety of operations exist in the prophetic office, the evangelistic office and the teaching office, so the apostle labors uniquely within the will of God for his own life. James was different from Paul, and Peter was quite unlike John. Although unity is essential, a precise uniformity in function among apostles is not.

The definition of an apostle needs to be approached free from erroneous mind-sets. Keeping in mind the marvelous duration, distinctions, dimensions, development and diversities of the apostle will help us maintain a stable foundation for understanding the definition of the apostle.

MEANING OF THE TERM APOSTLE

The word "apostle" sheds a great deal of light on the subject of the apostle's work and character. The original Greek word translated apostle is *apostolos*. It comes from a root word, meaning one who is sent forth or sent away from one place to another to accomplish a specific mission. The word "apostle" was used of men who were naval officers or merchant mariners responsible for an entire fleet of ships. It was also used to refer to an emissary or ambassador; to a fleet of ships or an expedition sent with a specific objective; to the admiral who commanded the fleet or to the colony that was founded by the admiral.

If a fleet of ships left Rome to establish a new colony somewhere, all of these were called apostles—the fleet, the admiral and the newfound colony. The particular truth emphasized by this usage is the relationship of those who were sent to the sender. All of these, the admiral, the fleet and the colony that was formed, represented the one by whom they were sent. In other words, they were faithful to transmit or reflect the intentions of the sender. The primary attitude of a true apostle, then, must be faithfulness.[10]

Apostles had the mission of overseeing the movement and task of these ships for long distances so that the objective of a higher authority could be accomplished. Apostles were in charge of overseeing resources, motivating and managing manpower, dealing with changeable circumstances and conditions and handling enemy forces in such a way as to please their superiors.

The term *apostolos* itself may be translated "messenger," or "one that is sent with orders." Apostles are delegates on a clear mission for an authority figure. They go forth as representatives of their commanders, sent to carry out their orders. The word "apostle" is prominent in the New Testament, occurring in every kind of New Testament writing: Gospels (10 times), Acts (28 times), Epistles (38 times) and the book of Revelation (3 times), for a total of 79 occurrences. A related term we have already discussed is *apostello*, which means *sent*. Apostles are simply "sent ones," as in Acts 13:1-4 (emphasis mine):

> Now in the church that was at Antioch there were certain prophets and teachers: Barnabas, Simeon who was called Niger, Lucius of Cyrene, Manaen who had been brought up with Herod the tetrarch, and Saul. As they ministered to the Lord and fasted, the Holy Spirit said, "Now separate to Me Barnabas and Saul for the work to which I have called

them." Then, having fasted and prayed, and laid hands on
them, they *sent* them away. So, being *sent* out by the Holy
Spirit, they went down to Seleucia, and from there they
sailed to Cyprus.

Another related term is *pempo*, translated as "sent," but it is used
only in John's writings. It is the rough equivalent of *apostello*, and is
used interchangeably to mean *sent*, as in John 13:16: "Most assuredly, I
say to you, a servant is not greater than his master; nor is he who is *sent*
greater than he who *sent* him" (emphasis mine).

Apostles are viewed in Scripture as church messengers:

If anyone inquires about Titus, he is my partner and fellow
worker concerning you. Or if our brethren are inquired
about, they are *messengers* of the churches, the glory of
Christ (2 Cor. 8:23, emphasis mine).

Yet I considered it necessary to send to you Epaphroditus,
my brother, fellow worker, and fellow soldier, but your
messenger and the one who ministered to my need (Phil.
2:25, emphasis mine).

Above all, we must keep in mind the picture that is painted of apostles in Ephesians 4, where they are seen as equippers given by Christ to
the Body to perfect and mature it.

CAN WOMEN BE APOSTLES?

This is a truly complicated question, but as Gilbert Bilezikian has pointed out, "every generation of Christians needs to examine its beliefs and
practices under the microscope of Scripture to identify and purge away
those worldly accretions that easily beset us, and to protect jealously
the freedom dearly acquired for us—both men and women—on the
hill of calvary."[11]

Some of the peripheral issues related to the question of women as
apostles will not be dealt with here. They include such questions as:
Can women speak in church? What is meant by submission, veils, covering and male headship? The answers involve complex grammatical

exegesis, and have been thoroughly dealt with by other authors. Our question is not one of women in ministry, but one of women in apostolic ministry.

Arguments Against Women as Apostles

Several long-standing arguments have been leveled against women as apostles. These can be summarized as follows:

The Bible establishes a pattern of all-male priesthood or ministry. Aaron and his sons were called by God to minister to God's people. Jesus chose men as His apostles. "Our Lord certainly foresaw that, as a result of His crucifixion, the Jewish priestly system would end. He could have taken that opportunity to break the mold of an all-male ministry if He had wanted to. That He did not do so speaks clearly against any sexual change and in favor of continuing the pattern of male priesthood."[12]

Due order prevents a woman from being in authority over a man. Because man was created first, and woman was created to be a "helper" (Gen. 2:18), a woman must not be allowed to exercise authority over men (see 1 Tim. 2:12). Man is the head of the woman (see 1 Cor. 11:2,3). Having women as apostles would violate the due order of male headship.

No examples of women as apostles are found in Scripture. In this regard, it is noteworthy that prominent champions of modern apostolic ministry often take a strong position against women as apostles. For example, Dick Benjamin, a forerunner in apostolic ministry, writes, "The gifts spoken about in Ephesians were given by Christ the apostle, Christ the prophet, Christ the teacher, Christ the master and head of the church, infusing His personality into five masculine ministries which were to lead the church into perfection. They are not valid ministries for women."[13] He also states that "Ruling is not a feminine function"[14] and that "women missionaries, single or married, are out of order in attempting to fulfill any of the ministries of an apostle."[15]

I know several men who lead great apostolic networks and churches that maintain these positions, or slight variations of them. They have wonderful ministries and defend their positions with sincerity and a deep appreciation for women.

Arguments for Women as Apostles

An equal number of reasonable arguments, however, are made to assert that women *can* be apostles. They include the following summarized positions:

Deborah is an example of a woman raised up by God and placed in a governmental position (see Judg. 4—5). She became a military commander and the governess of a nation. Though many say that God chose a woman only because men failed to fill the role, it is difficult to see how an omnipotent God could not find one man among tens of thousands in Israel that could suitably lead. In this case, God's choice to govern was a woman.

Women played vital roles in Paul's apostolic ministry. Don Williams notes, "The sharing of women in ministry calls forth the strongest affirmation from Paul. Phoebe has been a helper of the Apostle (Romans 16:2). Priscilla joined Aquila in risking her neck for Paul and all the churches are thankful for her (Romans 16:3-4). Mary worked hard among the Romans (Romans 16:6). Rufus's mother mothered Paul (Romans 16:13). Nympha has a church in her house (Colossians 4:15, [*NIV*]). Chloe's people report to Paul (1 Corinthians 1:11). Lois and Eunice have a sincere faith (1 Timothy 1:5, and Apphia is a sister in the Lord to Paul and Timothy (Philemon 2). It is exactly the incidental nature of these references that makes them all the more impressive. Paul loved, affirmed, and depended upon, and ministered with women. They are 'fellow workers' in the gospel."[16]

Scriptural and historical reasons lead us to believe that women can be involved in governmental as well as apostolic positions. Phoebe was noted by Paul as a "servant" (literally, *a minister*) of the church at Cenchrea, and a "succorer *(prostasis)* of many." As Patricia Gundry points out, the primary definition of prostasis is "a woman set over others."[17] This indicates a position of considerable authority.[18] Evidently she was able to comply with scriptural principles of authority, headship and covering while maintaining a position of oversight.

Junia was an apostle and was more than likely a woman. Charles Trombley writes:

> It is argued that Junia could be Junias, a man's name, but scholars aren't absolutely sure which gender is meant, since both the names Andronikos and Junias are in the accusative case. Rather than beginning from a base of uncertainty, it is possible to search the writings of the early church fathers

who were much closer to the original manuscripts and church than we are today.

John Chrysostom (337-407), bishop of Constantinople, wasn't partial to women. He said some negative things about women but spoke positively about Junia. "Oh, how great is the devotion of this woman that she should be counted worthy of the appellation of apostle!" Nor was he the only church father to believe Junia was a woman. Origen of Alexandria (c. 185-253) said the name was a variant of Julia (Rom. 16:15), as does *Thayer's Lexicon*, Leonard Swidler cited Jerome (340-419), Hatto of Vercelli (924-961), Theophylack (1050-1108), and Peter Abelard (1079-1142) as believing Junia to be a woman.

Dr. Swidler stated, "To the best of my knowledge, no commentator on the text until Aegidus of Rome (1245-1316) took the name to be masculine." Apparently the idea that Junia was a man's name is a relatively modern concept but the bulk of the best evidence available is that Junia was indeed a woman, and an outstanding apostle.[19]

Although women were not found among the Twelve, the Twelve were ordained as apostles to Israel where the presence of women in leadership would not have been accepted. We cannot reasonably argue that women cannot be apostles because they were not among the Twelve. They are two separate classes of apostles. Further, by using this faulty logic we would be able to argue that because no African men were among the Twelve, African men cannot be apostles, and so on. This kind of thinking would not be logical.

We cannot overlook the amazing words of the apostle Paul in 1 Thessalonians 2:6-8, where he describes his apostolic ministry in decidedly female terms such as nursing and cherishing. *The Amplified Bible* renders verse 7, "But we behaved gently when we were among you, like a devoted mother nursing and cherishing her own children." It is unlikely that Paul would have chosen such language if he had been afraid of combining the concepts of femininity and apostleship in the same context.

Given the evidence, we may reasonably conclude that women may serve Christ in governmental and apostolic positions if their gifting, character and proper relationship with God-ordained authority allow it, and if they are sovereignly called by God. Although it appears that this kind of ministry is possible, it also appears to be infrequent. Conservative openness is a wise position in the service of a God of order and sovereignty. Above all, this issue must never be allowed to polarize or divide the Body of Christ. People of goodwill and sincere faith can disagree about this point while maintaining the apostolic anointing and passion in their lives.

Whatever position one holds to, it is undeniable that women have been a key force in apostolic ministry in modern times. I shudder to think where we would be if all the women in history who have lived and worked as missionaries and overseers had not been allowed to do so. Kevin Conner, a noted author, eloquently states, "If ever women should find their place and find fulfillment, surely it should be in the redemptive and covenant community, the church."[20] Women are too gifted and too numerous to exclude from meaningful involvement in the important task of world evangelization and the emerging apostolic movement.

SEVEN DEMANDS THAT DEFINE APOSTLES

One way we get insight into the work of apostles is to understand what is required of them. A brief summary sheds light on who the apostle is.

1. *Apostles are required to have a definite and personal call from God in their lives.* As we have seen in chapter 3, this is essential.

2. *Apostles are required to have a special intimacy and acquaintance with Jesus Christ.* In 1 Corinthians 9:1, Paul qualifies himself as an apostle by citing his contact with Christ: "Am I not an apostle? Am I not free? Have I not seen Jesus Christ our Lord?" Clearly, personal acquaintance with Christ was considered a requirement for apostleship among the Twelve (see Acts 1:21-25). Although today's apostles are of a different category, we can be sure that intimate knowledge of Christ is vital for fruitfulness in apostolic ministry (see John 15:4,5).

3. *Apostles are elders and must meet the biblical qualifications of an elder.* A person cannot be an apostle if moral and spiritual requirements set forth for overseers in Scripture are not met (see 1 Tim. 3:1-7; Titus 1:5-9; 1 Pet. 5:1-4).

4. *Apostles are fivefold ministers and must function as such.* The work of a valid apostle will always be in the areas of equipping, training and

leading others into mature ministry. ("Fivefold ministry" is a widely used term that refers to the five ministries given by Christ to the Church to stand in unique spiritual offices, as found in Ephesians 4:11-17.)

5. *Apostles are required to have the recognition and confirmation of peers.* One thing that unnerves me as I consider the future of the apostolic movement is the likelihood that this office will come into abuse by unqualified people who assume a position for which they are not called. That is why I have included an entire chapter about "False Apostles" (chapter 10) and have in several places carefully described the biblical requirements for ordination and validation of apostles in their calling. Other apostles must recognize a person as an apostle before apostolic ministry can be entirely legitimized (see Gal. 2:9; Acts 13:1-3). In this era of self-proclaimed ministries, we would do well to remember these important principles of balance and safety.

6. *Apostles must have specific fruit* to which they can point to demonstrate their apostleship. In 1 Corinthians 9:1,2, where Paul's calling was challenged, he pointed to established lives and churches as proof positive of his calling. Apostleship is not a mystical state of mind; it is an actual ministry that can be measured in the tangible terms of established churches, spiritual children in the ministry and penetrating the gospel into targeted areas.

7. *Apostles must maintain their apostleship by complete submission to Christ,* or they will fall from apostleship and lose their office as did Judas (see Acts 1:25).

Keeping all these scriptural parameters in mind, we have defined an apostle as *a person who is called and sent by Christ and has the spiritual authority, character, gifts and abilities to successfully reach and establish people in Kingdom truth and order, especially by founding and overseeing local churches.*

Peter Wagner offers this excellent definition of an apostle:

> The gift of apostle is the special ability that God gives to certain members of the Body of Christ to assume and exercise general leadership over a number of churches with an extraordinary authority in spiritual matters that is spontaneously recognized and appreciated by those churches.
>
> Apostles are those whom God has given especially to pastors and church leaders. They are those to whom pastors

and church leaders can go for counsel and help. They are peacemakers, troubleshooters and problem solvers. They can make demands that may sound autocratic but that are gladly accepted because people recognize the gift and the authority it carries with it. They have the overall picture in focus and are not restricted in vision to the problems of one local church.[21]

DEFINITION WITHOUT PERSONALIZATION

Though it has been a difficult decision, I have deliberately chosen *not* to provide my readers with a list of examples of modern-day apostles in this book, and I would like to explain why. I must confess that trying to define a ministry as complicated and relatively unexplored as apostles has not been easy. For that reason, such a list would possibly be helpful in bringing us above the fog of confusion that surrounds this ministry. By providing names of people whom I might view as apostles, however, an entirely new set of problems would arise that would muddy the waters and jeopardize the influence of this message to the Church. I am not providing names for the following five reasons:

1. As far as I know, God has not charged me with the responsibility of saying who is an apostle and who is not. All I can do is make some suggestions based on my personal opinions. The Lord ultimately knows what He has called each person to be. I do not care to stand in the place of a self-appointed and sole judge of true apostleship!

2. Because the office of apostle has not yet come into widespread acceptance, many whom I might list would not acknowledge that title as appropriate for themselves and thus become uncomfortable. Little would be gained by this uneasiness.

3. Such a list might further polarize people of differing perspectives when what we need is agreement. If I personalize my definition of an apostle, depending on whom I name, some may react against that person's theological position, ministry style or other "baggage" that would produce confusion, or maybe an outright rejection of the idea of modern apostles. For example, if I suggest the name of a particular charismatic, many of my dear noncharismatic readers might find it difficult to swallow, and move away from the message of this book. That would be tragic, in my view. If I fail to mention a particular apostle,

some may take that as my rejection of that person's calling. Again, people might split about an issue that should bind us together.

4. The suggested names would have to be leaders of wide recognition and renown to be meaningful to most of my readers. In listing such names, we run the risk of implying that all apostles are famous—another possible misconception. Many legitimate yet still emerging apostles might think that true apostleship is linked to a level of recognition unattainable for them, and become discouraged in the pursuit of their calling. I have sought in this book to bring wider acceptance and encouragement of this ministry, not to discourage it.

5. I do not believe this book is the place for such a list. A different kind of study would be required to identify such people. It is my intention, the Lord willing, to write a follow-up to this book that would focus on profiling a variety of nationally and theologically diverse apostles so as to shed more light in this area.

For these reasons, I am planning not to cloud the issue by giving personalizations, which might bog down the discussion. Rather, I would like to provide for my readers the biblical pattern so we can begin to accept and practice apostolic ministry. I am content to simply define apostleship, and leave the personalizations to the reader.

A clear definition of terms can do wonders to help the Body of Christ rise out of the fog of ignorance into the clear light of God's Word about apostles and apostolic ministry. Despite the darkness the enemy has introduced, apostles are both needed and indicated for today. If we fail to break out of confusion and regain our scriptural bearings, we can never rise to fulfill the high calling that is upon us in this hour: the call to *planting and watering for increase.*

Notes
1. Vinson Synan, "Who Are the Modern Apostles?" *Ministries Today* (March/April 1992): 42.
2. Wayne Grudem, *Systematic Theology, An Introduction to Biblical Doctrine* (Grand Rapids: Zondervan Publishing House, 1994), p. 911.
3. Ed Murphy, *Spiritual Gifts and the Great Commission* (Pasadena: William Carey Library, 1975; currently out of print), p. 197.
4. Ibid.
5. Ibid.

6. C. Peter Wagner, *Your Spiritual Gifts Can Help Your Church Grow* (Ventura, Calif.: Regal, 1979; revised edition, 1994), p. 181.

7. Ibid.

8. Stanley M. Burgess and Gary B. McGee, eds., *The Dictionary of Pentecostal and Charismatic Movements* (Grand Rapids: Zondervan, 1988), pp. 95-96. My thanks to Bayard Taylor for his suggestions about this point.

9. Bill Scheidler, *The New Testament Church and Its Ministries* (Portland, Oreg.: Bible Temple, 1980), p. 90.

10. Ibid., p. 88.

11. Gilbert Bilezikian, *Beyond Sex Roles* (Grand Rapids: Baker, 1985), p. 214.

12. Bernard E. Seton, "Should Our Church Ordain Women? No." *Ministry* (March 1985): 16.

13. Dick Benjamin, "Here's What the Bible Says About Women's Ministries," *The Gospel Truth* (July/August 1980): 9.

14. Ibid., p. 10.

15. Ibid., p. 12.

16. Don Williams, *The Apostle Paul and the Women in the Church* (Van Nuys, Calif.: Bim Publishing, 1977), p. 144.

17. Patricia Gundry, *Woman Be Free!* (Grand Rapids: Zondervan, 1977), p. 102.

18. Richard Clark Kroeger and Catherine Clark Kroeger, *I Suffer Not a Woman* (Grand Rapids: Baker, 1992), p. 91.

19. Charles Trombley, *Who Said Women Can't Teach?* (South Plainfield, N.J.: Bridge Publishing, 1985), pp. 190-191.

20. Kevin J. Conner, *The Church in the New Testament* (Australia: Acacia Press, 1982), p. 229.

21. C. Peter Wagner, *Your Spiritual Gifts*, pp. 181-182.

7

PLANTING AND WATERING FOR INCREASE

RECOGNIZING *who an apostle is* REQUIRES UNDERSTANDING *what an apostle does.* Apostleship begins with a person's heart and character, but culminates in action. Apostles must experience a total fusion of their convictions and their conduct—bringing their hearts together with their hands—if they plan to consummate their calling.

If we want to see the ministry of the apostle fully restored today, we need to grasp the nature of the apostle's job. What are the particular passions of an apostle, and in what kind of activities will an apostolic person be involved? How did the apostles go about their work in Scripture, and how can we achieve the same kinds of results?

TWO ASPECTS OF APOSTOLIC MINISTRY

Though Scripture reveals a wide variety of personalities among apostles, a marvelous uniformity exists in the work they do. Whether their calling is to Jew or Greek, their overall functions are the same: *apostles are seasoned and fruitful harvesters.* Their lives are consumed with the passion of planting and watering for increase.

Apostolic ministry may be difficult and demanding, but it is not mysterious. Everything an apostle does can be understood as either *planting* or *watering.*

Using these words, Paul offered a beautiful allegory of the work of an apostle. He wrote to the church at Corinth, which he had founded:

> Who then is Paul, and who is Apollos, but ministers through whom you believed, as the Lord gave to each one? I planted, Apollos watered, but God gave the increase. So then neither he who plants is anything, nor he who waters, but God who gives the increase. Now he who plants and he who waters are one, and each one will receive his own reward according to his own labor. For we are God's fellow workers (1 Cor. 3:5-9).

Planting

Paul depicts planting as breaking new ground. He wants us to understand that apostolic work means establishing new life. The apostle is seen as a gardener, a cultivator of spiritual life.

How do apostles plant? They begin by selecting a fertile soil. It has to be a place where abundant fruit will be produced. The land must then be cleared by prayer, and the soil must be turned over with diligence. They then sow the seed of the Word of God into the soil of people's hearts. Because they sow in tears, they know they will reap in joy (see Ps. 126:5). Truth begins to take root in the people, and after a time, new life emerges.

What do apostles plant? They plant churches. The pattern throughout the book of Acts is simple—apostles are sent to penetrate cities and found local churches. The late Dr. William Steuart McBirnie states this case simply, yet profoundly: "Having traced their lives very carefully, from every scholarly source obtainable, this writer has concluded that without exception the one thing the Apostles did was to build churches—not buildings of course, but congregations. As far as the record reveals, in each city or populated area where some accepted the Gospel, the Apostles established a congregation."[1] After coming home to rest and report, they revisit their works and then move on to other fields where the process is repeated.

Planting churches requires a constant sensitivity to the will of God. Timing is essential, and planting is a seasonal thing (see Eccles. 3:2). The Holy Spirit reserves the right to direct His servants as they go (see Acts 16:6-8). We must also remember that the Lord of the harvest has no obligation to bless anything He has not initiated. "Every plant which My heavenly Father has not planted will be uprooted" (Matt. 15:13).

Watering

By watering, Paul speaks of carefully nourishing and sustaining that which has been planted. Apostles are ongoing sources of strength and refreshing to the work they have planted. Using the water of the Word, they skillfully impart the nourishment of truth, irrigating the souls of the thirsty with precepts that produce faith and strength. As the refreshing impartation is soaked up, the work grows stronger.

Paul taught at Antioch, nourishing those who were there for an entire year (see Acts 11:26). He remained at Corinth for 18 months, watering the converts there with the Word (see 18:11). Paul stayed at Ephesus, teaching daily for two solid years at the school of Tyrannus (see 19:9). His total stay at Ephesus lasted three years, the balance being spent teaching day and night (see 20:31).

Once a church plant becomes capable of sustaining itself, the apostle moves on. As F. F. Bruce observed, "When those churches had received sufficient teaching to enable them to understand their Christian status and responsibility, the apostle moved on to continue the same kind of work elsewhere."[2] Presumably, at that point in time, the work would be handed over to the local leadership.

Though this can be demanding work, none of it permanently depletes the apostle's spiritual supply, for God has promised that "the generous soul will be made rich, and he who waters will also be watered himself" (Prov. 11:25). Though apostolic work is taxing, God is faithful to replenish the reserves of those who give their very best.

Apostolic churches also replenish themselves. In God's amazing vineyard, that which is watered ultimately becomes a source for further planting. "For as the rain comes down, and the snow from heaven, and do not return there, but water the earth, and make it bring forth and bud, that it may give seed to the sower and bread to the eater" (Isa. 55:10). One local church plant can produce future apostles, prophets and pastors. The church can also furnish the finances necessary to support new works.

THE GOAL OF INCREASE

In apostolic ministry, the goal of all planting and watering is *tangible increase.* Apostles plant and water because they want to present a harvest to the Lord. Their aim is not to be known as apostles; they want to be perennial producers of changed lives in an expanding Kingdom.

The early days of the Church were considered nothing if they were not days of outstanding increase and harvest. As the Word was preached with power, a miraculous and constant multiplication of converts came forth to form a great company of believers (see Acts 6:7). Acts records that "the churches were strengthened in the faith, and increased in number daily" (16:5).

The apostles' productivity helps to certify their authenticity. "Am I not an apostle? Am I not free? Have I not seen Jesus Christ our Lord? Are you not my work in the Lord? If I am not an apostle to others, yet doubtless I am to you. For you are the seal of my apostleship in the Lord" (1 Cor. 9:1,2). Part of the proof of the apostles' calling is an established people. Apostles who do not save souls and establish churches are like farmers who do not produce a harvest.

Increase is imminent whenever God is involved. He desires to bless what we plant because He loves us. As Israel prepared to cross the Jordan and enter the Promised Land, Moses promised the nervous settlers: "And He will love you and bless you and multiply you; He will also bless the fruit of your womb and the fruit of your land, your grain and your new wine and your oil, the increase of your cattle and the offspring of your flock, in the land of which He swore to your fathers to give you" (Deut. 7:13). We must never allow our fear of failure to keep us from planting and watering. God *will* give us the increase if we follow His lead.

PRINCIPLES OF INCREASE

How does increase occur? God has given us certain universal principles to tap into and utilize to produce increase. These principles need to be meaningfully applied in the emerging apostolic movement so that dynamic increase can come to the Church.

Increase comes from investment. Apostles invest their lives, their finances and their time. When we sow in ministry, we shall reap a harvest of results. "There is one who scatters, yet increases more; And there is one who withholds more than is right, But it leads to poverty" (Prov. 11:24).

Increase rises through faith. Apostles move in faith for increase. They teach faith to their people, knowing that this results in an extension of the scope of their ministries (see 2 Cor. 10:15). "So the churches were strengthened in the faith, and increased in number daily" (Acts 16:5).

Increase follows effort. Apostles are not afraid of hard work. "Wealth gained by dishonesty will be diminished, but he who gathers by labor will increase" (Prov. 13:11). A true apostle is like a mighty ox that rarely tires and brings forth great increase (see 14:4).

Increase comes through synergy. Apostles understand the importance of united, widespread and effective participation from the people of God. It took Paul *and* Apollos to water and plant. Every part of the Body must be active, contribute and be in harmony for increase to occur (see Eph. 4:16; Col. 2:19). (More will be said about this principle in chapter 14, "The Kingdom Net.")

Increase is a reward for obedience. Apostles understand the blessings of obedience to the heavenly vision (see Acts 26:19). The blessing outlined for those who obey the Word of God is increase (see Deut. 28:4).

VEHICLES OF APOSTOLIC MINISTRY

Now that we understand the principles of planting, watering and increasing, we come to the question: *What vehicles do apostles use to perform these essential functions?*

Whether apostles are in the process of planting or watering, *effective communication* is central to their work. Apostles continually communicate truth, bringing forth doctrine, reproof, correction and instruction from the Word of God (see 2 Tim. 3:16). They are to teach, preach and minister in the Spirit. If this is not done effectively, apostles can never fulfill their ministries.

Apostles can use two primary vehicles to communicate truth effectively:

1. *Vocal ministry.* Apostles use their mouths to share and communicate. They spend hours teaching, preaching and prophesying. Apostolic work is verbal work, and the apostle needs a ready mouth. Paul urged the Ephesians to pray, "That I may open my mouth boldly to make known the mystery of the gospel" (Eph. 6:19).

2. *Written ministry.* The apostles distributed epistles and messages to their churches when they could not be there personally, keeping in touch through paper and ink (see Acts 21:25; Gal. 6:11; 1 Pet. 5:12;

1 John 2:21). Some of these communiqués are the Scriptures we use today. Although the Scriptures are complete, apostles still need to write down their lasting record of important truths for the benefit of others. Many apostles in the emerging apostolic movement will be writers and will need to hone their skills as authors.

THE SEVEN RESPONSIBILITIES OF AN APOSTLE

Apostles must be prepared to embrace other responsibilities. These form the entire framework for the practical side of apostolic ministry, and give shape to the actual work of planting and watering.

Planting Churches

Apostles plant local churches because these churches are the building blocks of the Kingdom. As they plant, they are responsible for imparting the faith and laying a proper foundation for dynamic growth (see Eph. 2:20). Apostles are church planters (see Acts 13:4—14:26). This aspect of the apostolic function is most easily recognized as perennial.

Ed Murphy notes the late Ray Stedman's comment: "It is part of the apostolic gift to start new churches. We call those who do this 'pioneer missionaries' today. In the course of Church history, there have been many such secondary apostles, as Adoniram Judson in Burma, William Carey in India, Hudson Taylor in China, etc. *These were men who had the apostolic gift and were made responsible for imparting the whole faith to new churches*" (Stedman, 1972: 72).[3] Over a period of time, these churches are structured with proper government, doctrine and practices.

The work of planting a local church involves penetration into new territory. Paul made it his aim to preach where others had not preached. He wanted to reach the unreached (see Rom. 15:14-24). As apostles plant new churches, they must also serve as able pastors and evangelists to win souls and bring people to maturity in Christ.

The apostles of the New Testament normally chose to plant churches in strategic city centers, not remote places. Of the apostle Paul, for example, noted British author Roland Allen said, "All the cities, or towns, in which he planted churches were centres of Roman administration, of Greek civilization, of Jewish influence, or of some commercial importance."[4] If Paul were alive today, he might very well plant churches in major cities such as Jakarta, Tokyo, Calcutta and Cairo, as well as San Francisco, Chicago and New York.

The modern apostle needs to follow the forms of the apostle of the first century, laying proper foundations, reaching the unreached and concentrating on strategic centers of population.

If apostles plant churches, what kind of churches do they plant? For insight into the kind of churches apostles should plant, see chapter 13, "Patterns for Apostolic Churches."

Overseeing and Strengthening Churches

Apostles carry a deep love and concern for their churches (see 2 Cor. 11:28). They know that once a church has been planted, it must be nurtured and protected to ensure its survival. Apostles guard their harvest, frequently checking up on the converts in an effort to see them established in Christ (see Acts 15:36). If they cannot personally visit their church, they will send representatives (see 1 Cor. 4:17). Apostles rejoice when they see proper order and an established faith in their churches (see Col. 2:5-7).

These responsibilities require the presence of certain spiritual giftings. A grace for structuring and administration is required to handle the needs of a growing assembly. A strong pastoral ability will help to protect and lead the sheep. Apostles will have the mantle of teacher as well, for they are concerned about proper doctrine, and want truth established with precision (see Acts 2:42; 15:1-31).

Developing Leaders

A great portion of the apostles' time is spent in establishing new leaders (see 2 Tim. 2:22). This is the guarantee of continuing increase in the apostles' harvest. Apostles must serve as fathers and teachers, producing spiritual children, as Paul did with Timothy and Titus. These spiritual offspring can assist them in apostolic work. Apostles will also be concerned about supplying local church pastors, elders, deacons and workers to fully support the house of God.

Faithful apostles avoid developing overdependence on their leaders, for they know they will not stay in one place forever. They aim instead to establish a successful process of discipleship whereby strong people are set up to serve the church when the apostle leaves for another place of planting.

Ordaining Ministries

Once apostles have poured themselves into faithful servants, they will set these servants into church offices. Apostles will regularly ordain elders and deacons to rule and serve in the house of God (see Acts 6:1-6; Titus 1:5).

During these times, apostles may assemble a prophetic presbytery to lay hands on those who are being ordained. Together, this team of ministers will impart spiritual gifts to the candidates (see Rom. 1:11; 1 Tim. 4:14; 2 Tim. 1:6), along with accompanying prophetic words (see 1 Tim. 1:18). Ordination is a solemn responsibility and calls for adequate preparation through fasting and prayer (see Acts 14:23).

Supervising and Coordinating Ministries

A large part of the apostle's responsibilities includes filling the role of a ministry manager. Because of the great responsibilities involved as overseers, apostles must be able to act as administrators, utilizing people to get things done. The apostles I have known are constantly brokering solutions and matching people to places and needs.

Along these lines, apostles will have frequent need of faithful representatives who can fix problems and fill positions. Paul recruited Timothy in Lystra and took him on apostolic journeys (see Acts 16:1-4). He later sent Timothy to various places in his stead for ministry responsibilities (see Phil. 2:19,20). Tychicus was also sent to various places to assist in Paul's absence (see Col. 4:7-12).

This kind of activity calls for the supernatural grace of God upon the apostle's life. The gift of administration is essential here (see 1 Cor. 12:28). The skills related to delegation, oversight and proper accountability will assist the apostle in managing ministry successfully.

Managing Crisis

Apostolic work is filled with problems, and apostles can be understood largely as problem solvers. Economic crises, leadership issues and violations of proper practice and conduct will routinely require the attention of the apostle.

The apostles addressed the need for famine relief in the Early Church (see Acts 4:34-37; 11:29,30). They were involved in the lives of those who fell into sins that required church discipline (see Acts 5:1-11; 1 Cor. 5; 2 Cor. 2:5-11). They took action in the doctrinal divisions that arose in the Church (see Acts 15:1-6). Much of the work of apostles consists of continually setting things in order (see 1 Cor. 11:34).

Networking with Other Ministries

When the apostles came together in the Jerusalem Council, they left for us an example of the importance of collegiality in ministry. No balanced apostle seeks to be isolated from others. Apostles who separate themselves and avoid fellowship with other ministers are manifesting poor character and should be considered suspect (see Prov. 18:1).

In the Body of Christ, no one individual ministry has it all. We need one another (see 1 Cor. 12:21). A true apostle has this understanding and wants to spend time growing through association and strengthening the Church through efforts of cooperation and unity. These efforts will involve building relationships with a wide spectrum of movements and people within the Body of Christ. Again, we'll talk more about this in my final chapter, "The Kingdom Net."

SUMMARY

To retrace what we have seen, consider the outstanding verbs we have used to articulate the work of an apostle: *establishing* and *nourishing* the Church. The vehicles by which the apostles carry their work forward include *communicating, teaching, preaching* and *writing*. The apostle's list of responsibilities includes: *overseeing, strengthening, developing, imparting, fathering, ordaining, supervising, managing* and *networking*. These words define not only what apostles do, but also who they are.

If we could ask the apostle Paul to summarize the apostolic calling, he would probably offer an array of glowing words to explain his many roles as a teacher, laborer and servant of Christ. He might repeat his tender words to Corinth about his daily concern for all the churches (see 2 Cor. 11:28). He would likely mention the sufferings he had survived and the abundance of revelations God had given him.

More than anything, I am persuaded that Paul's description would not conclude before he had spoken joyfully and passionately of the real work of an apostle and the apostolic people who work with him: *planting, watering* and *increasing*.

Notes

1. William Steuart McBirnie, *The Search for the Early Church* (Wheaton, Ill.: Tyndale House, 1978), pp. 27-28.
2. F. F. Bruce, *Paul: Apostle of the Heart Set Free* (Grand Rapids: Eerdmans, 1977), p. 315.
3. Ed Murphy, *Spiritual Gifts and the Great Commission* (Pasadena: William Carey Library, 1975, currently out of print), p. 201.
4. Roland Allen, *Missionary Methods, St. Paul's or Ours?* (Grand Rapids: Eerdmans, 1962), p. 13.

8

THE SIGNS
OF AN APOSTLE

FOR THOUSANDS OF YEARS, WHENEVER THE AUTHENTICITY OF PRECIOUS
metal needed to be determined, the touchstone was employed. Using
this method, the metal in question would be rubbed against the touchstone—a smooth black glossy stone—which always told the truth. The
marks the metal left on the touchstone would be compared to the
touch-needle (a genuine sample of the metal in question), and a determination would be made. If the metal was genuine, its mark would be
identical in color and luster to the touch-needle. If there was any difference, the metal would be immediately rejected. This provided a universally accepted way to test gold and silver. Whenever there was a
question, the touchstone settled matters conclusively.

TRYING AN APOSTLE

In our quest to understand apostles and apostolic ministry, we need to
ask if there is such a touchstone test for apostleship. Can the authenticity of apostolic ministry be examined and determined so as to
remove any doubts?

These are days in which it will be imperative to assess the validity of
apostleship. Unfortunately, a proliferation of flaky apostolic impostors
will likely accompany the apostolic movement. Second Corinthians
11:13 warns us that false apostles exist who are "deceitful workers,
transforming themselves into apostles of Christ." The Holy Spirit spoke

to the leader of the church of Ephesus and commended him saying, "I know thy works, and thy labor, and thy patience, and how thou canst not bear them which are evil: *and thou hast tried them which say they are apostles, and are not, and hast found them liars*" (Rev. 2:2, *KJV*, emphasis mine). Spotting and dealing with false apostles is the subject of chapter 10. For now, let's consider the idea that apostles can be tried in the Spirit and shown to be genuine or not, and the important basis of that test.

THE SIGNS OF AN APOSTLE

Although no physical touchstone exists that tries apostles, it is possible to determine whether or not a person is a genuine apostle. Just as silver and gold are known for their natural qualities, apostles can be known by their spiritual qualities. Certain qualities that Scripture points to indicate true apostolic character and ability. Paul himself had to refer to them to validate his own calling and identity before the church at Corinth. In doing so, he left us with a silhouette of apostleship to which we refer in our search for clarity:

> Truly the signs of an apostle were wrought among you in all *patience*, in *signs*, and *wonders*, and mighty deeds (2 Cor. 12:12, *KJV*, emphasis mine).

The New International Version has translated the phrase the *King James Version* interprets as "signs of an apostle" to read "the things that mark an apostle" (2 Cor. 12:12). These signs are literally tokens or indications that mark the presence of an apostolic calling and grace upon a life.

What are the signs of an apostle? Paul describes three: patience, signs and wonders, and mighty deeds. Patience relates to the heart and character of an apostle, and signs and wonders have more to do with that person's gifting and spiritual abilities. Each of them deserves our keen attention. We will deal with the first and most important quality—patience—in this chapter. Signs, wonders and mighty deeds are the subject of chapter 12, "Apostles and Supernatural Power."

THE MARK OF PATIENCE

Paul spoke of the first sign of an apostle as "patience." This is an important concept we must carefully understand. At first, when we ponder the traits of an apostle, our minds are likely to be filled with images of preaching to the lost, raising the dead, planting churches and other such demonstrations of spiritual power. We probably would not choose patience as a sign of true apostleship. But the New Testament marks of an apostle *begin* with this far-less-spectacular, but far-more-important, character quality of patience.

From God's perspective, character comes first in apostolic ministry. Signs, wonders and mighty deeds have their place to be sure, but having those graces and abilities in operation without the presence of character would be useless as well as harmful. Although many today seek to validate their ministries by pointing out the miracles and mighty deeds, we know that God is still looking at their hearts before He gives His approval. First Samuel 16:7 reminds us that "the Lord does not see as man sees; for man looks at the outward appearance, but the Lord looks at the heart." Jesus Himself received the full approval of the Father before He ever performed His first miracle (see Matt. 3:16,17). In apostolic ministry, character is foundational.

Recently I had the pleasure of meeting a great man whom I had not seen in more than 15 years. Dr. Costa Deir is from Jerusalem, and has spent his life tirelessly traveling the nations of the world as an apostle. Sensing the divine opportunity, I sought his input for this book. I asked him, "Costa, whom do you see on the world scene today that you would say shows the marks of a true apostle?" Frankly, I expected him to give me a quick answer. Instead, he cocked his head and squinted his eyes, as if in deep reflection.

In his unique Middle-Eastern accent, he replied, "I would have to really think about that before answering." Then he really dropped the bomb: "Forgive me, but you Americans are always looking for the outward marks of ministry in order to make a quick association with a title. But apostleship is first an internal quality. We easterners look at the character and the things inside an individual that define who he is."

At that moment, I knew he had shared an essential truth of apostleship I would never forget: Apostleship is a matter of character above any other single quality.

Of the many possible signs of an apostle's authenticity, patience is wisely chosen by the Holy Spirit as the first mark on the touchstone.

Patience embodies the concept of proven character more than any other quality because having patience implies not only character, but a character that has been tested in difficulty and proven over a period of time. Consider Romans 5:3,4, which teaches us to "glory in tribulations also: knowing that tribulation worketh patience; and patience, experience [literally, approved character]" (KJV). Patience is a seal that validates a person's spiritual authenticity.

UNDERSTANDING PATIENCE

What is patience, and why is it so essential in apostolic work? When we first think of patience, we might think of waiting patiently for an important letter to arrive in the mail, or waiting patiently for a traffic light to turn green. The kind of patience for which the apostles were noted is a totally different thing. The Bible delineates patience as remaining persistent in the face of opposition. When a soldier in the thick of the battle, encountering enemy bombs and bullets flying all around, stays at the post instead of going AWOL, that is patience. When a sentry who is responsible for guarding something valuable stands alone in the cold night as the rain and wind prevail, but is not moved, that is patience. Patience is staying anchored when everything around is drifting off course. It is manning a station and fulfilling a duty no matter what.

When the apostle Paul was faced with the imminent loss of his life, his testimony to the Ephesian elders was, "None of these things move me; nor do I count my life dear to myself, so that I may finish my race with joy, and the ministry which I received from the Lord Jesus, to testify to the gospel of the grace of God" (Acts 20:24). Paul's words demonstrate patience in the biblical sense.

The Greek word in 2 Corinthians 12:12 for patience is *hupomone*, which means a cheerful endurance. It comes from a root word meaning to remain intact under pressure or difficulty. The virtue of patience is highly praised throughout the New Testament as a mark of the highest integrity, ranking with other admirable characteristics such as godliness, faith and love (see 1 Tim. 6:11; 2 Tim. 3:10; Titus 3:2). The author of Hebrews views life in Christ as a race and encourages us to run the race and finish victoriously with this kind of steady endurance (see Heb. 12:1).

PATIENCE REQUIRED IN SUFFERINGS

Patient endurance in the life of an apostle is especially necessary in light of the constant exposure of that office to hardship and suffering. What kind of suffering goes with apostolic ministry? The apostles in the book of Acts were threatened, falsely accused, beaten, imprisoned, stoned and even beheaded. For these experiences they rejoiced that they were worthy (see Acts 5:40-42). When they weren't facing immediate death, they had to travel by the most primitive methods, face hostile authorities, defend their apostleship, stand up to unfriendly pagans and battle demonic forces. They viewed themselves as virtual slaves to Christ, enduring a life of hardness and brutal sacrifice (see 1 Cor. 4:9-13).

As He spoke prophetically to the apostles about the tribulation of the last days, Jesus warned them that the quality of patience would be necessary. They would be tested by great persecution:

> Then they will deliver you up to tribulation and kill you, and you will be hated by all nations for My name's sake. And then many will be offended, will betray one another, and will hate one another. Then many false prophets will rise up and deceive many. And because lawlessness will abound, the love of many will grow cold. But he who endures to the end shall be saved (Matt. 24:9-13).

APOSTLES WILL SUFFER

The affliction Christ saw coming upon the Church would occur in the context of apostolic ministry. Although the apostles fulfilled the ministry of preaching the gospel to all nations, resistance would develop. Being delivered in this would require endurance (see v. 13). Those who lacked patience in this difficult season would fall away, betray one another and be influenced by false prophets.

This was not the only time Christ called His apostles to endurance. In Matthew 10:5-22, Christ is outlining the apostolic mission of the twelve in preparation for sending them to the lost sheep of the house of Israel. He commands them to heal the sick, cleanse the lepers, raise the dead and cast out demons. He charts out how they should operate. He also warns them that they will be persecuted, saying:

Behold, I send you out as sheep in the midst of wolves. Therefore be wise as serpents and harmless as doves. But beware of men, for they will deliver you up to councils and scourge you in their synagogues. You will be brought before governors and kings for My sake, as a testimony to them and to the Gentiles. But when they deliver you up, do not worry about how or what you should speak. For it will be given to you in that hour what you should speak; for it is not you who speak, but the Spirit of your Father who speaks in you. Now brother will deliver up brother to death, and a father his child; and children will rise up against parents and cause them to be put to death. And you will be hated by all for My name's sake. But he who endures to the end will be saved (Matt. 10:16-22).

Again, patience and endurance are the keys to being saved in the midst of these difficulties.

Christ's prophecies of the apostles' suffering proved accurate. Besides enduring the most difficult persecutions while alive, traditional statements tell us that most of the apostles died as martyrs. Matthew died in Ethiopia by the sword. Mark was cruelly dragged through the streets of Alexandria and expired because of his wounds. Luke was hanged by the neck in Greece. Peter was crucified upside down in Rome. James the Greater was decapitated in Jerusalem. James the Lesser perished after being thrown from a pinnacle of the Temple and beaten on the head with a fuller's club. Bartholomew was skinned alive. Andrew was crucified. Thomas was impaled with a lance in the East Indies. Jude was shot to death with arrows. Matthias was first stoned and then beheaded. Barnabas was stoned. Paul, the apostle, met his death by being beheaded in Rome by the psychopathic Nero. Only John escaped the cruelty of martyrdom, though it was attempted. He was put in a cauldron of boiling oil, but was miraculously protected. Later banished to Patmos, he was released and died of natural causes.[1]

THE APOSTLE PAUL'S PATIENCE IN MINISTRY

Patience in the apostolic service of Jesus was nothing new to Paul, though he was not numbered with the twelve. He encountered spiritual attacks, natural discomforts of every kind, religious persecutions and finally martyrdom—all because he was an active apostle. His insights into persecution and difficulty include these comforting words:

> Now if we are afflicted, it is for your consolation and salvation, which is effective for enduring the same sufferings which we also suffer. Or if we are comforted, it is for your consolation and salvation (2 Cor. 1:6).

Consider the catalog of character qualities demonstrating Paul's apostolic authority in 2 Corinthians 6:4-10, and notice the point and counterpoint between the patience and suffering woven within the fabric of his ministry:

> But in all things we commend ourselves as ministers of God: in much patience, in tribulations, in needs, in distresses, in stripes, in imprisonments, in tumults, in labors, in sleeplessness, in fastings; by purity, by knowledge, by long-suffering, by kindness, by the Holy Spirit, by sincere love, by the word of truth, by the power of God, by the armor of righteousness on the right hand and on the left, by honor and dishonor, by evil report and good report: as deceivers, and yet true; as unknown, and yet well known; as dying, and behold we live; as chastened, and yet not killed; as sorrowful, yet always rejoicing; as poor, yet making many rich; as having nothing, and yet possessing all things.

The apostle Paul details some of the suffering necessitating his own exercise of steady endurance. He faced labors, floggings and imprisonments. He was stoned and beaten. In addition to the catastrophic experiences already cited from 2 Corinthians 6, he encountered various other perils, including shipwreck. He experienced every possible form of emotional pain, weariness and exhaustion. Hunger and thirst, cold and nakedness, and intense concern for the churches were all his frequent companions. Paul faced immeasurable pressures, beyond his ability to describe, and despaired of his own life on occasion, but stood in his calling without wavering (see 2 Cor. 1:8-10; 11:23ff).

Any one of these experiences would be enough to cause the immature to retreat, but true apostles are marked by steady endurance under pressure. That kind of character keeps the apostolic ministry moving forward.

PASSING THE TEST

Doubtless this was the very quality of patient endurance Paul looked for in the life of John Mark. When Paul and Barnabas determined to return to the cities they had preached in and confirm the disciples and converts there, Barnabas believed that John Mark should accompany them. Paul, however, strongly disagreed because he had abandoned them in Pamphylia, presumably at the prospect of difficulty (see Acts 15:37-39). He could not, or would not stand firm when adversity presented itself. It must have seemed to Paul that John Mark was a quitter. Paul so adamantly rejected him as a team member that a dispute arose between him and Barnabas, resulting in them separating. Paul was taking a firm stand regarding the issue of character, because he felt strongly about it. No sharper conflict exists in the New Testament between fellow laborers than between these two apostles.

Was Paul overly concerned with John Mark's inability to endure? We must remember how important patient endurance is in apostolic ministry. The younger John Marks in the Body of Christ cannot be depended upon to stand firm under pressure and difficulty. It is too easy for them to quit. The prospect of pain and sacrifice causes them to waiver and wilt. Further development is necessary so that one day they can qualify, as John Mark did, to stand profitably with the apostles (see 2 Tim. 4:11).

THE TOUCHSTONE OF CHARACTER

How can we determine an apostle's authenticity? Long before we look at charisma, we must examine character. We must strike the touchstone of patience against the character to see if the quality and purity required for apostolic ministry are present. Apostolic ministry and suffering are inseparably entwined, and those who answer the apostolic calling must be prepared to face difficulty with a mastery of it. Without this ingredient in place, the apostle (and the whole apostolic movement) will not endure.

God is raising up apostles and apostolic people in this hour who understand how to patiently endure suffering. They will be able to withstand pressure and pay the full price for apostolic ministry. They understand that the apostolic calling will mean sacrifice and suffering, but their character is such that they embrace it joyfully because on their touchstone they have the greatest mark of all: *the mark of the prize of the high calling of God* (see Phil. 3:14).

Note
1. Paul Lee Tan, *Encyclopedia of 7,700 Illustrations: Signs of the Times* (Rockville, Md.: Assurance Publishers, 1979), pp. 333-334.

A MOVEMENT OF
THE FATHERS

FROM OUT OF THE DESTINY-DRENCHED EARLY DECADES OF THE CHURCH comes a story of affection and faith that still inspires and instructs us today. It is a story about how God uses spiritual fathers to transform history by touching young people who want to be transformed. It is the story of Paul and his young companion, Timothy.

Life for Timothy began in Lystra, a Roman colony in Galatia, located just northwest of Tarsus and southeast of Antioch. Timothy was an unassured young man, timid and, at times, fragile. His mother was a devout Jewess, his father a worldly Gentile who likely did not nurture Timothy's interest in the things of God. Because his father had little expertise in matters of religion, it was devout women who figured prominently in the formation of Timothy's faith. That influence made him *aware of God*, but it seems that he never became *alive in God* until he met a devout man—a man who became a father in a way Timothy had never known.

Paul came to Lystra paired up with the apostle Barnabas, and together they ministered with life-changing apostolic power. Through them a crippled man was healed that day, and the inhabitants of that city were so overcome with amazement that they fell at the feet of the apostles to worship them as gods. The Jews from Antioch and Iconium quickly turned the crowds against the two preachers, and Paul was mobbed, stoned and left for dead.

Later Paul returned to Lystra and encouraged his converts to face tribulation using faith. Little did Timothy know as he heard those words that day that he would need to live by them as he experienced the exciting and difficult life of traveling with an apostle. Five years later, Paul would return again and find Timothy ready to begin his ministry. The two men united, and a new team emerged to change the world.

Paul was a dominant and positive force in the life of Timothy. He led Timothy to Christ, though the seeds had already been planted by his mother Eunice, and his grandmother Lois (see 1 Tim. 1:2; 2 Tim. 1:5). Paul introduced him to active ministry by taking him along on an apostolic journey that would influence his spirit forever (see Acts 16:3). Together they wrote to churches, preached, taught converts, faced dangers and experienced a powerful bond of affection. Paul laid his hands on Timothy and spoke life over him (see 1 Tim. 4:14). Everything Paul had within himself the Holy Spirit also poured into Timothy. He was his father in the faith (see Phil. 2:22).

The story of Paul's love and how it transformed Timothy becomes a classic study in the significance of spiritual fathering. We now direct our attention to this area, which is intrinsic to apostleship, and which will figure prominently in the emerging apostolic movement.

THE IMPORTANCE OF FATHERS

Fathering is essential to success at every level of society. Sociologists are now confirming that fathers not only play an indispensable role in the home, but also in the nation. Many of the problems we face in America today—drugs, welfare, teenage pregnancy—are directly related to the absence of fathers throughout the past several decades. Fatherlessness is the most destructive trend of our generation. The absence of fathers is linked to most social nightmares. Social scientists have made similar links between a father's absence and his child's likelihood of being a dropout, jobless, a drug addict, a suicide victim, mentally ill and a target of child sexual abuse.[1] Any home or nation lacking the presence of the father is dreadfully weakened.

Why? Because fathers bring strength and stability to these environments. Take the family, for example. Without fathers, children are more likely to grow up undisciplined and irresponsible, unaware of consequences in life. Fathers bring a strong standard and a firm hand that enables a family to reach its potential. When storms come, good fathers steady the ship with their wisdom and experience. They bring balance to the family system. The strength of a father provides tremendous protection for a family's future and ultimate destiny. *Spiritual fatherlessness* is a weakness in the Body of Christ today; a great vacuum has been created by the scarcity of godly fathering. Like society, the Church is plagued with problems. We need the same kind of discipline and accountability a natural father brings to a natural family. We need wisdom and maturity, a firm hand to guide us, balance to preserve us and experience to comfort us. Noted pastor and author Frank Damazio laments the current crisis of fatherlessness permeating the Body of Christ. "Today young leaders search desperately for models they can imitate and look up to. Today's leaders live when heroes have flaws and fail and when dreams have died. When religious systems are corrupt and modern ministry does not offer a mentoring model, young leaders may end up following wrong models."[2] Without spiritual fathers, the Church cannot achieve its ultimate destiny.

I predict that in the coming apostolic outpouring, a restoration of spiritual fathering will materialize, filling this void and releasing a *movement of the fathers*. Because the same qualities essential to families are needed in the family of God, a new generation of spiritual fathers will be enlisted by the Holy Spirit. They will bring their stability and strength not only to the movement, but also to the entire Body of Christ. The apostolic movement will bring spiritual fathers to their places in the house of God, and spiritual fathers will help protect the movement from extremes and errors.

Before I go any further I want to state that my use of the terms "father" or "fathering" should not be misunderstood to mean that I am excluding women from vital mentoring roles in the emerging apostolic movement. Timothy's life, for example, was deeply affected by his mother and grandmother (see 2 Tim. 1:5). I have adopted the biblical motif of fathers because it is so pronounced in Scripture. Both men and women will make a significant contribution to this movement, each in their own unique ways. The principles I share here can be adapted to work among spiritual mothers and their children.

APOSTLES AS FATHERS

Where will we get these needed fathers? Along with other ministries (such as the pastor), the apostle will take on the mantle of a father in and through this coming movement. One of the most striking characteristics of an apostle's ministry is spiritual fatherhood. Apostles father by facilitating growth and development of God's family just as natural fathers care for their families.

Look at the apostle Paul's fatherly words to the Church at Thessalonica:

> Nor did we see glory from men, either from you or from others, when we might have made demands as apostles of Christ. But we were gentle among you, just as a nursing mother cherishes her own children. So, affectionately longing for you, we were well pleased to impart to you not only the gospel of God, but also our own lives, because you had become dear to us. For you remember, brethren, our labor and toil; for laboring night and day, that we might not be a burden to any of you, we preached to you the gospel of God. You are witnesses, and God also, how devoutly and justly and unblamelessly we behaved ourselves among you who believe; as you know how we exhorted, and comforted, and charged every one of you, *as a father does his own children*, that you would walk worthy of God who calls you into His own kingdom and glory (1 Thess. 2:6-12, emphasis mine).

Just as the Old Testament family of God had many regal patriarchs—honorable, wise, strong—so God is giving the New Testament family of God spiritual fathers in the form of seasoned apostles and other fivefold gift ministries. God is raising up another generation of patriarchal men who possess the kind of wisdom, respect, and leadership necessary to guide and oversee the family of God in these otherwise aimless days.

Of course, not every spiritual father is an apostle. Many great pastors have exercised the ministry of spiritual fatherhood with excellence, apart from an apostolic calling. But we cannot neglect the fact that the apostles in the Bible were uniquely regarded as spiritual fathers. An abundance of insight is available to us as we see them in that light.

Restoration of the Fathers

God works through fathers. In the final moments of this age, when God will work as never before, we can expect that He will use spiritual fathers. In the final words of the Old Testament, a unique prophet saw a glorious vision of the end-time move of God's Spirit:

> Behold, I will send you Elijah the prophet before the coming of the great and dreadful day of the Lord. And he will turn the hearts of the fathers to the children, and the hearts of the children to their fathers, lest I come and strike the earth with a curse (Mal. 4:5,6).

These restored father-son relationships will be mirrored in spiritual father-son relationships in the Kingdom. God will restore this important position to the family of God so that the Body of Christ will receive the love, training, provision, reproduction and impartation He has ordained. The Paul-Timothy relationships of Scripture will again be a living reality in the Church!

It is exciting to consider the potential effect of restoring the spiritual father within the Church. In a day when we are continually confronted with the tragic results of lives lacking the benefits of fathering, and where the father's absence is seen to be the source of many emotional problems, restoring spiritual fathering will breathe fresh life and hope into the Church.

How Fathers Function

Fathering is a skill that needs to be taught and imparted copiously as the apostolic movement evolves. "The world has the service of thousands of erudite scholars, but the Church is still crying out for the ministry of the spiritual fathers."[3] Despite their great love for the Lord and desire to be productive, many spiritual men still lack the ability to act as spiritual fathers. The breakdown of fatherhood within our society is one reason for this. When we grasp some of the main functions of fathering, and allow these functions to operate within the Church, many lives will be changed by thoroughly skilled apostolic fathers.

At least five similarities between the apostle (or any spiritual father) and a natural father open our eyes to the function of a New Testament spiritual father. Understanding these functions will not only help us to prepare the way for spiritual fathers, but it will also assist us in recognizing them as they appear.

1. Fathers Demonstrate Love

Fatherhood and love are inseparable concepts in the plan of God. The love relationship between a father and his son provides the ideal environment for training and developing the character and life of the son. Without love, a son may grow, but he cannot flourish.

Fathers nurture their children, affectionately caring for them. They affirm their children and provide the gentle security of an unwavering commitment to their well-being. They give themselves to their children, opening their lives like a book of rare wisdom to share with them. A man who cannot share himself in love may be a biological progenitor, but he is not a spiritual father.

Few relationships can surpass the love a father has for his son. This level of devotion is seen in Jacob's relationship with his son Benjamin. As Jacob's heart and mind—his very life—were involved in the life of his son Benjamin (see Gen. 44:30), so any godly father's life is knit together with the life of his son— heart with heart and soul with soul. God required father Abraham to lay his son Isaac on the altar. This requirement was a metaphor of God's own father-heart toward Abraham. God knew this was an illustration of love with which Abraham could identify. The love that God the Father has for His Son, Jesus Christ, is the ultimate example of the intensity of the love God has ordained between fathers and sons (see John 3:35; 5:20; 10:17).

Apostles are vessels filled with immense love. True apostles cherish their spiritual children as Paul did when he said he was "affectionately desirous...willing to have imparted...not the gospel of God only, but also our own souls, because ye were dear unto us" (1 Thess. 2:8, *KJV*). His message to the Corinthians was equally passionate when he wrote: "I speak not this to condemn you: for I have said before, that ye are in our hearts to die and live with you" (2 Corinthians 7:3, *KJV*).

Dick Iverson, who oversees a large network of churches, has eloquently observed, "An apostle does not just set up an 'empire of churches' over which he reigns and from which he receives glory and honor. Instead, the charge of all the local churches that God gives him becomes a gut-wrenching, intensely emotional, heartfelt, passionate ministry of life to precious souls! It is an awesome responsibility. It is not an arms-length transaction. The apostle must feel the very heartbeat, the pulse of the church, and be in touch with the lives of its people."[4]

Is this dimension of devotion important? Without fatherly affection, the apostle could become an overbearing and oppressive influence in the Church. With the quality of sacrificial love, his care mirrors that of the heavenly Father, overseeing people using the sensitivity and skill that makes him an irreplaceable asset.

2. Fathers Train and Discipline

Essential in the endeavor of raising mature and well-adjusted children is the art of training them. Fathers take a powerful part in this process, firmly directing and guiding their children into activities and attitudes that will prepare them for success. Any man can get a woman pregnant, but it takes a true father to raise his children and impart the proper training and preparation for life to them.

Fathers direct their children into productive paths. Jethro, the wise father-in-law of Moses, offered direction to his overworked son-in-law that both preserved and protected him in the face of crushing responsibilities (see Exod. 18:13-26). Joseph's counsel to Pharaoh was so effective that he was promoted to the place of positional fatherhood over him (see Gen. 45:8). Even great men need the direction of a father.

A true father accepts responsibility for his children. The biblical role of a father is to raise his children to a place of maturity and fruitfulness: "And, you fathers, do not provoke your children to wrath, but bring them up in the training and admonition of the Lord" (Eph. 6:4). This is rarely easy, and can also be unpleasant. It involves countless confrontations between the father and his son for instruction, adjustments, correction and discipline. The heart of a father is committed to enduring any lengths to develop maturity in his offspring.

God Himself is a father who disciplines and trains His children. The writer of Hebrews reminds us:

> And you have forgotten the exhortation which speaks to you as to sons: My son, do not despise the chastening of the Lord, nor be discouraged when you are rebuked by him:

For whom the Lord loves He chastens, and scourges every son whom he receives. If you endure chastening, God deals with you as with sons; for what son is there whom a father does not chasten? But if you are without chastening, of which all have become partakers, then you are illegitimate, and not sons. Furthermore, we have had human fathers who corrected us, and we paid them respect. Shall we not much more readily be in subjection to the Father of spirits and live? For they indeed for a few days chastened us as seemed best to them, but He for our profit, that we might be partakers of His holiness. Now no chastening seems to be joyful for the present, but painful; nevertheless, afterward it yields the peaceable fruit of righteousness to those who have been trained by it (Heb. 12:5-10).

Just as natural fathers train and discipline their children, and just as the Father trains and disciplines us as His children, so the apostles and other spiritual fathers must train and develop their children for spiritual maturity.

As an apostle, Paul fathered many sons (see 1 Cor. 4:14). At various times we can observe his gentle guidance, firm correction and detailed instruction of them. He modeled ministry before the people of God. He demonstrated and explained truth in the hope of influencing people as a father hopes to impact his sons. His goal as an apostolic father was to present everyone under his care before Christ, mature and complete (see Col. 1:28). His ministry extended beyond that of a teacher into the realm of a spiritual father because he was committed to the responsibilities of training his spiritual offspring.

3. Fathers Provide

Another primary task of a father is to provide for his children. Proverbs 13:22 states that a good man provides not only for his children, but for his children's children. Paul wrote to the Corinthians that he planned to provide for his own material needs saying: "Now for the third time I am ready to come to you. And I will not be burdensome to you; for I do not seek yours, but you. For the children ought not to lay up for the parents, but the parents for the children" (2 Cor. 12:14). Fathering and provision are inseparable.

To "provide" means to sustain and enrich. A true father gives all that is necessary to his children to maintain and improve their lots in life. The prodigal's father so wanted to provide for his son that he was willing to give him his inheritance early even if it meant he would leave home (see Luke 15:12). Our heavenly Father gives us every good gift (see Jas. 1:17), and because of His great love for us, He willingly sacrificed His only Son (see John 3:16).

What does a spiritual father provide for his spiritual children? What is the inheritance he leaves? A legacy of spirit can only come from a spiritual father to his spiritual children. As Elijah ascended in the chariot of fire, Elisha received his mantle—symbolic of his anointing and prophetic office—amid his cries of grief: "My father, my father!" (2 Kings 2:12) The most valuable heritage a spiritual father can leave his child is to impart his own spiritual drive and ability. Men such as Paul give young men such as Timothy things far beyond any earthly inheritance. They leave for them heavenly legacies of effectiveness, anointing and passion for God.

4. Fathers Reproduce

In the most basic sense, natural fathers are men who have physically contributed to creating a new life. They are men who have biologically reproduced.

Apostles are considered fathers because they create and establish things. They exercise the powers of spiritual reproduction, planting churches and creating ministries wherever they go. They give spiritual life to new children in the faith by becoming the vessels through which those children enter into the new birth. They continue their ministries as fathers by raising up and reproducing their own ministries within such lives. Apostles are spiritual fathers who possess reproductive abilities. As spiritual fathers, apostles carry the seed of the next generation within their lives. They propagate and populate the kingdom of God through their ministries. That is why this ministry of duplication within spiritual fathers is essential to the life and vitality of the Church, and is yet another reason apostles are so desperately needed today.

5. Fathers Bless and Impart

Of all the functions of fathering, the spiritual blessing and oversight of the family may be the most forgotten and neglected in our day. Many fathers understand well how to love, provide for and train their children, but many lack the ability the Old Testament patriarchs and the great apostolic fathers of the Early Church profitably exercised—imparting spiritual blessing.

Consider the poignant stories of the Bible patriarchs and prophets imparting to their children. In the story of Jacob and Esau, Jacob so coveted his father's blessing that he tricked the aging Isaac into giving it to him instead of Esau. How precious was that blessing, and how desperately Esau sought it afterward! It is amazing to consider that both desperately sought their father's blessing, even though they were fully mature men.

Later on, Jacob would lay his hands on his son Joseph's children and bless them. Jesus also laid His hands upon children, recognizing that little sons and daughters need to be touched and blessed (see Mark 10:16). Though fathers today seldom practice blessing their children, we must understand the power involved in it as we minister to both our natural and spiritual sons.

The New Testament has much to say about the importance of a father's blessing. The apostle Paul pictures God the Father blessing us as His children with all spiritual blessings through our relationship with Christ (see Eph. 1:3). Jacob's blessing of Joseph's sons becomes a picture of faith for the believer (Heb. 11:21). As fathers to their spiritual children, the apostles who wrote the Scriptures were careful to open and close their letters by imparting a spiritual blessing to their readers. The apostle Paul laid his hands on his spiritual son Timothy and was used to impart gifts and blessings that Timothy was responsible to utilize (see 2 Tim. 1:6).

Apostolic fathers have the ability to impart blessings to their children in the faith. This transference of divine life is one of the most awesome responsibilities of a spiritual father. Speaking from experience, I can say that this is one of the greatest experiences any spiritual son can have.

DIMENSIONS OF SPIRITUAL FATHERHOOD

Fatherhood is a complex process including several potentially significant applications in the Church. Exactly how will spiritual fathers function in the emerging apostolic movement? What part will they play in this visitation?

Spiritual fathers will exercise their ministries in two primary dimensions: corporate and individual. In each of these areas, the Church needs light.

1. Fathers over the House of the Lord

The first level of authority is corporate authority, where an apostle heads up a group of people or ministries that relate to him as a father. This group of people could be referred to figuratively as a "house" or "tribe." The local churches for which Paul had apostolic oversight, for example, would have him as their spiritual father (see 1 Cor. 9:2). Though not everyone within these churches would have been closely acquainted with Paul, they were still submitted to him as a spiritual father. The message and tone of his letter to these churches suggests that Paul understood this to be true: "For though you might have ten thousand instructors in Christ, yet have you do not have many fathers; for in Christ Jesus I have begotten you through the gospel" (1 Cor. 4:15). This kind of apostolic oversight can be found in many places today, and will multiply in the emerging apostolic movement.

This dimension is preshadowed in the Old Testament where the patriarchs were set over households and tribes. In tribes, the entire exchange of authority, inheritances, relationships and resources were all arranged according to families.

God's people have always been managed and led within households of spiritual authority, led by father figures. Abraham was a patriarch to a household of thousands whose faith still speaks to us today (Gen. 17:5). He has become a pattern for all believers, and is considered the father of our faith. Isaac, his son, became a patriarch, and gave birth to Jacob, whose sons fathered the 12 tribes, or households, of Israel. Moses certainly became a father figure to the house of Israel as they wandered through the desert. The entire Old Testament narrative is built around the households and families of the lineage of Christ and God's dealings with these households. Likewise, as God continues to turn the hearts of the fathers and children toward each other in this hour of outpouring, we shall see New Testament patriarchs caring for different spiritual families in the form of spiritual fathers.

The New Testament is full of language describing spiritual tribes and households within the family of God. The apostle James refers to the saints as "the twelve tribes which are scattered abroad" (Jas. 1:1). Jesus Himself points to leaders over spiritual households in the powerful illustration of the two servants (see Matt. 24:45,46; Luke 12:41-48). The teaching portrays the Lord at His second coming, where He desires to find faithful and wise spiritual leaders ruling their "households." Here they are distributing "food in due season" or pure and timely spiritual provisions for those in their care. Christ is opposed to evil men who misuse their positions and abuse their households. Galatians 6:10 directly refers to the Body of Christ as the "household of faith," and Ephesians 2:19 refers to the Church as the "household of God." Satan's spiritual kingdom is also described as a household governed by a head householder (see Matt. 10:25; 12:25,29,44).

In a real sense, any fellowship of believers or churches resembles an Old Testament family tribe or household. Each tribe had a patriarchal head who shared his identity and personality with the tribe. Many of the patriarchs ruled with the assistance of elders, and carried out purposes unique to their tribe, but normally in harmony with the other tribes that made up the nation. The entire household looked up to the father figure for insight, direction and covering. These same dynamics exist in healthy New Testament churches, such as the Abbott Loop Christian Fellowship based in Anchorage, Alaska. Dick Benjamin, the overseer, refers to his network as a "family of churches" sponsoring an annual conference referred to as a "family reunion."[5] This reflects the security and closeness that God provides for His people as He "sets the solitary in families" (Ps. 68:6).

The apostolic fathers of the New Testament governed their church households by using a parental tone. The apostle Paul's second letter to the church of Corinth includes the corrections, consolations and scoldings of a father responsible for a household. Both the apostles John and Paul referred to their readers as "my little children" (Gal. 4:19; 1 John 2:1; 3:18).

God has ordained that churches and fellowships of ministries be led by men who have father's hearts. They will lead in conjunction with pastors and elders, and will set the group's unique identity and flavor. The conglomeration of all these tribes makes up the spiritual nation of the Church. More will be said about this as we examine the patterns of authority evident in apostolic structures. For now it is sufficient to grasp the concept of figurative households, tribes and patriarchs as they relate to the apostolic ministry.

2. Fathers over Sons in the Gospel

We have already alluded to the second dimension in which fathers will flow in the approaching apostolic stream. It is the realm in which a spiritual father relates to a spiritual son or daughter. This kind of fathering takes place on an intimate and individual level rather than on a corporate level; it is the dimension of mentoring.

A renewed interest is occurring in the subject of mentoring because it is essential in human development. In the apostolic movement, this level cannot be overlooked. It is the key to developing the many thousands of apostles God is calling forth in this hour.

In this regard, the Biblical term "beget" becomes important. Scripture is filled with passages describing family lines—records of who begat whom. The word beget speaks of causing to become, which is distinct from simply giving birth. Although the important and irreplaceable role of mothers should not be minimized, it is interesting that mothers do not beget. In Scripture, it is the father that causes his children to become something. This is another aspect of the power of fathering. It is the essence of being a spiritual father of a son or daughter in the Gospels. The spiritual father begets, causing his spiritual son or daughter to become something in God. This intensifies our appreciation of Jesus being the "only begotten" of His father (John 1:14,18; 3:16,18).

The father-son relationship must be protected and valued. Exodus 20:12 commands us to honor our fathers that our lives may be long. The father has a preserving effect on the spiritual children. Old Testament law provided that if a son struck or cursed his father, he would be put to death. A death begins to work in any son or daughter who rejects a father—natural or spiritual. Tragic results always occur when a father-child relationship is interrupted. Like children who raise themselves, the separated spiritual child may become rude, unmannerly and self-serving.

A MIGHTY SON RAISED UP

As we have seen, Paul considered Timothy his dear son in the faith. He fathered Timothy in the faith, and mentored him in ministry. Did Paul's investment in young Timothy pay off?

Through the power of spiritual fathering, a world-changer was born. Paul's affection moved Timothy from the place of preparation to the place of maturity, from spiritual boyhood to spiritual manhood. Tradition tells us that after Paul's death, the once-timid Timothy became the distinguished overseer of the great apostolic church at Ephesus, and a prominent spiritual father himself. Once a simple young follower, Timothy became a leader of many followers. The legacy of apostleship would continue because of spiritual fathering.

The apostle is a father, and in the emerging apostolic movement, more spiritual fathers will emerge. They will exercise love, discipline, provision, reproduction and blessing in the house of the Lord and their sons in the gospel. An entire generation of modern Timothys who stand ready will be mentored and released to change the world. Houses of faith will grow into mighty tribes; sons in the faith will become men of the Spirit, and the process will multiply with quantum force. As it does, curses will be broken and the gospel will penetrate the hearts of men. The people of God will grow and mature as never before, and the kingdom of God will flourish because this movement is a movement of the fathers.

Notes

1. Joseph P. Shapiro, Joannie M. Schrof, Mike Tharp and Dorian Friedman, "Honor Thy Children," *U.S. News and World Report* (February 27, 1995): 39.
2. Frank Damazio, *The Vanguard Leader* (Portland, Oreg.: Bible Temple, 1994), p. 17.
3. Frank Damazio, *The Making of a Leader* (Portland, Oreg.: Bible Temple, 1980), p. 56.
4. Christian Equippers International, *The Master Builder* (1985): 77.
5. Ibid.: 179.

FALSE APOSTLES

FOR THE APOSTLES, THE DAYS FOLLOWING THE RESURRECTION OF JESUS WERE marked by both excitement and crisis. None of them fully expected Christ to rise from the dead. They had heard Him speak of it, but the agony of calvary was such that it seemed their hopes had been despairingly dashed. How could Jesus recover from the cross and the grave that followed? When they discovered He had risen, unimaginable joy and relief flooded their hearts. As Christ ascended to the Father, they prepared to tell the world the good news!

The apostles' intense excitement about the risen Christ was no doubt tempered by their lingering memory of the fallen apostle, Judas Iscariot. This man, who had been numbered with the apostles, had coldly betrayed Christ into the hands of His oppressors. Judas's grief was immediate and unbearable; he hung himself and plunged to a violent death in a pool of blood. His suicide was as tragic as his betrayal, and the painful memories of that scene haunted these men.

Later, as the apostles and followers gathered in the Upper Room in Jerusalem, Peter sensed the concern that gripped them all. How could they tarry and pray for the coming of the Spirit with this incident still on their minds? They had gnawing questions: *How could they have been fooled? Had Judas always been a fake? If so, why would Christ have chosen him? How could an apostle fall?* They tried to make some sense of it all.

Furthermore, Jesus had appointed 12 apostles, but since the death of Judas Iscariot, only 11 remained to do the job. What should be done?

Finally, Peter rose to address the somber group. He cited the psalms that prophetically foretold the penalty of Judas's sin: "Let their dwelling place be desolate; let no one live in their tents" (Ps. 69:25); "Let his days be few, and let another take his office" (109:8). A curse was upon Judas according to the Word of the Lord, and he was not to be pitied. His office was to be given to another.

The apostles would forge ahead. The twelfth office would stand, and another man would be selected to fill it. He would be one more witness of the Resurrection, standing with the apostles, and completing the number Christ had ordained. After prayer, Matthias was selected, and a bright era began to dawn for the apostles. The wind rushed, the fire fell and the Church breathed its first breath.

We cannot address the subject of what a true apostle is without considering the false apostle's work. In this chapter we will look at the false apostle's work, doctrine, tactics and makeup, based on a wide variety of Scriptures.

A COUNTERMOVEMENT OF FALSE APOSTLES

Because the true apostolic movement will be a glorious and genuine outpouring of God's power on earth, it will not escape the enemy's attempts to counterfeit it. Frank Damazio has rightly pointed out that "every generation has its share of insidious impostors who pretend to know how to build churches but who in fact weaken them."[1] While authentic apostolic activity increases, Satan will endeavor to infect this movement with a countermovement of deceivers who claim true apostleship, but are not sent by God. Modern-day Judas Iscariots, driven by malevolent spirits, will attempt to mix in with true apostles in an attempt to bring ruin.

Satan's chief aim through these false apostles will be threefold: to *dilute, defile* and *discredit* the apostle and the apostolic movement. Many will be bewitched into rejecting true apostles because of the inevitable failures of false apostles. Critics of apostolic ministry will likely point out the problems of the false apostles in an attempt to dismiss the validity of apostolic activity. This effort may well become the single greatest threat to the apostolic movement's success.

It is essential that the countermovement of the enemy against the apostolic movement be properly anticipated and dealt with according to Scripture. The battle lines of apostolic ministry will be drawn—a lot will be at stake.

Critics of apostles and the apostolic movement will be quick to point out the extremes of false apostles to discredit the entire apostolic movement. Discerning people who truly desire a genuine move of God on earth, however, will look beyond the counterfeits to the genuine and see the reality of what God is doing. In this regard, truth is the essential ingredient. Armed with the clear understanding of the difference between true and false apostles, we will stand in the heat of the coming conflict without becoming casualties ourselves.

WHAT IS A FALSE APOSTLE?

But what I do, that I will do, that I may cut off occasion from them which desire occasion; that wherein they glory, they may be found even as we. For such are *false apostles*, deceitful workers, *transforming themselves into the apostles of Christ*. And no marvel; for Satan himself is transformed into an angel of light. Therefore it is no great thing if his ministers also be transformed as the ministers of righteousness; whose end shall be according to their works (2 Cor. 11:12-15, *KJV*, emphasis mine).

The Greek term for "false apostles" here is *pseudapostolos*, meaning those who masquerade as apostles, but are not. This word occurs only one time in Scripture.

It speaks of impostors who have a motive to gain by deceit, and Paul seems to want to reduce our shock at their existence. In effect, he says: "Don't be surprised if Satan sends impostors who look genuine." False apostles, then, are hell's attempt to imitate a true apostle for destructive purposes.

Paul spoke out against those who boasted falsely in their apostleship. Paul identified men who were false apostles by drawing attention to their motives for financial gain. To underline the difference between himself and the false apostles, he refused to accept finances from the Corinthians for a time so that he could show his superiority over those who take money in the guise of apostleship.

Paul also calls them "deceitful workers," revealing their skills at deception. Evidently the attraction of money drew these men into masquerades of ministry.

THE BROADER PROBLEM
OF FALSE MINISTRY

When we discuss false apostles, we are really dealing with the broader subject of false ministers of every kind. False leadership is a problem dealt with throughout Scripture. The false ministers of Pharaoh battled with God's true servants Moses and Aaron, and were able to duplicate many of their miracles and demonstrations of spiritual power. Balaam's name is synonymous with ministry tainted and motivated by money. The Old Testament prophets decried the false priests and shepherds of their day. Paul is particularly strident in his attacks against false ministers in the New Testament.

It is essential that we acknowledge the source of all false ministry as Satan himself. Paul said: "And no wonder! For Satan himself transforms himself into an angel of light" (v. 14). In this statement, Paul links the work of false apostles with something beyond mere error: he links it with hell itself. This fact must guide the Church in its response to false apostles today.

God has graciously provided the Church with gift ministries in the form of true apostles, prophets, evangelists, pastors and teachers. Note again their purpose as stated by Paul:

> And He Himself gave some to be apostles, some prophets, some evangelists, and some pastors and teachers, for the equipping of the saints for the work of ministry, for the edifying of the body of Christ, till we all come to the unity of the faith and of the knowledge of the Son of God, to a perfect man, to the measure of the stature of the fullness of Christ (Eph. 4:11-13).

Then note the following verse, and compare it to what he has already stated:

> That we henceforth be no more children, tossed to and fro, and carried about with every wind of doctrine, by the *sleight*

of men, and cunning craftiness, whereby *they lie in wait to deceive* (v. 14, *KJV*, emphasis mine).

Impostors will always surround the fivefold ministry. Paul speaks of true ministers, and immediately refers to their opposition to the false. We are being equipped so we will not fall prey to the false ministries that are always prowling around the Body of Christ, seeking to attack and injure.

SATAN'S COUNTERFEIT MINISTRY GIFTS

For every blessing God has ever created, Satan has presented a counterfeit. The ministry gifts of Ephesians 4:11 are no exception, and in this context we must understand false apostles. Because Christ has given the Church the apostle, prophet, evangelist, pastor and teacher, Satan (as a *false Christ,* see 2 Cor. 11:4) has created five crude and dangerous imitations to impersonate them:

1. Jesus warned us of *false prophets* that would appear in sheep's clothing, but inwardly were ravenous wolves (see Matt. 7:15).
2. Jesus spoke of *false shepherds* (or false pastors) who would come to kill, steal and destroy as hirelings. They would fail to protect the sheep, and instead would scatter and abandon them (see John 10:10-13).
3. The apostles Paul and Peter both warned of the existence of *false teachers* who would peddle fables and heresies to bring swift destruction to God's people (see 2 Tim. 4:3,4; 2 Pet. 2:1).
4. It is clear that *false evangelists* can be identified as those who spread a false gospel (see Gal. 1:9).
5. Jesus spoke to the angel of the church at Ephesus (to whom Paul wrote of the true gift ministries) of *false apostles*—men who were liars, claiming apostleship though they were not sent by God (see Rev. 2:2).

The counterfeit nature of these men may flow from one of two corrupt fountains. Some false apostles are false because they are apostates, that is, they have fallen away from a once-legitimate faith (see 2 Thess.

2:3). Like Judas, they begin by having a valid experience with God, but because of internal weaknesses, turn away from Christ to a life marked by error. The connection of the words "apostle" (one who is sent) and "apostate" (one who is fallen) is interesting in this regard. We may assume that some false apostles are total impostors who have *never* had an experience with Christ. In either case, they are regarded as deceived and dangerous people encouraged by the devil to bring harm to people.

DAYS OF DECEPTION

This kind of false ministry is an increasing problem in the world today. People still shudder at the memory of the tragic fruit of the false ministries of Jim Jones and the People's Temple, or David Koresh's Waco, Texas, compound. Increasingly, the New Age phenomenon is coming together with erring students of Christianity who blend the Bible with psychology and occult philosophy to spawn counterfeit ministries. Deception seems rampant, and many people's faith is faltering. This is exactly what Christ foretold would occur in the last days when he said,

> "Take heed that no one deceives you. For many will come in My name, saying, 'I am the Christ,' and will deceive many. And you will hear of wars and rumors of wars. See that you are not troubled; for all these things must come to pass, but the end is not yet. For nation will rise against nation, and kingdom against kingdom. And there will be famines, pestilences, and earthquakes in various places. All these are the beginning of sorrows. Then they will deliver you up to tribulation and kill you, and you will be hated by all nations for My name's sake. And then many will be offended, will betray one another, and will hate one another. Then many false prophets will rise up and deceive many. And because lawlessness will abound, the love of many will grow cold. But he who endures to the end shall be saved. And this gospel of the kingdom will be preached in all the world as a witness to all the nations, and then the end will come" (Matt. 24:4-14).

Although the effects of false ministry are horrid, we are reassured of the ultimate triumph of the Church. The gospel of the Kingdom will be preached around the world, and the harvest will be reaped!

All false ministry has common roots, so we shall examine false apostles within the scope of false ministers in general. Each Scripture we examine will depict one aspect or another of false ministry, and by extension, false apostles in particular. We will begin by examining what is at the heart of false apostleship.

FORCES AT WORK DEEP INSIDE THE FALSE APOSTLE

How does a Judas come to be a betrayer? For any man to come to this kind of horrible deception, some dark dynamics must be at work deep within him. Just as counterfeit watches sold on sidewalks may look like expensive Swiss timepieces, yet inside are cheap and unreliable, the inward workings of false apostles reveal the true story. Within the heart of every false apostle, some truly disturbing forces are at work.

We might imagine a variety of reasons for false apostles doing what they do, but only two major motives are mentioned in Scripture. Unlike much of modern psychology, the Bible does not excuse deviant behavior upon discovery of some childhood trauma or environmental deficiency. False apostles participate in their evil practices either out of the *love of money* (see Titus 1:11; Rev. 2:14; 2 Pet. 2:1-3) or the *sin of pride* (see 1 Tim. 6:4,5).

That money should be the root of this evil is not surprising. It appears that Judas was affected by this power himself. Great profit can come from the gifts of naive people who are told they are giving to God. Through manipulation, control and false practices, false apostles can tap the deep resources within their reach.

The motive of pride affected Lucifer himself (see Isa. 14:12-15) and resulted in his hideous transformation; it is also the basis of all of his activity at present. Doubt, division and deception are the by-products of a heart filled with a desire for gain and a prideful passion for power.

APOSTLES, MONEY AND INTEGRITY

Discussing the love of money as a motive in false apostles leads us to consider the question, *What is a true apostle's attitude toward money?* At first, this may seem to be a trivial question, but the Bible places a great emphasis on handling money properly, especially when it comes to ministry. Jesus indicated that money is an excellent reflection of a person's true inward motive, saying, "For where your treasure is, there your heart will be also" (Luke 12:34). The way a person handles money indicates the condition of the heart.

At issue is integrity. Integrity is the quality of aligning conduct with what is morally right—integrating right believing with right action. False apostles have no integrity, and so their attitude toward money is corrupt. Once someone can be trusted with money—and is walking in financial integrity—that person can be trusted with the spiritual riches of the Kingdom. Jesus declared: "Therefore if you have not been faithful in the unrighteous mammon, who will commit to your trust the true riches? And if you have not been faithful in what is another man's, who will give you what is your own?" (Luke 16:11,12). Integrity, as it is reflected by a person's uprightness concerning money, is an absolute plumbline between the false apostle and the true apostle.

True apostles have integrity at work in their lives, which is expressed in their proper attitudes and conduct toward money. When the early Christians sold their houses and lands, and laid their life savings at the feet of the apostles, they had no reason to fear any impropriety. The money would be used correctly (see Acts 4:35-37). A false apostle, however, would have mishandled the money. When Simon the sorcerer attempted to bribe the apostles into giving him the power of the Holy Spirit, Peter rebuked him sharply for his actions, discerning his bitter motive and his darkened heart. A false apostle would have gladly accepted the offer as a "love gift." A true apostle has the integrity of Paul concerning money, who was able to report to the Ephesian elders, "I have coveted no one's silver or gold or apparel" (Acts 20:33).

The coming apostolic visitation will be a true visitation of God's power flowing through people who are true blue when it comes to money. The Judas generation of false ministers cannot be allowed to corrupt this stream. The practices of twisting Scripture for financial gain, high-pressure offerings, lavish lifestyles and lack of financial accountability have no place in this movement. We must learn to recognize and defeat the spirit of Balaam before it can infiltrate what God has ordained to be pure.

IDENTIFYING A FALSE APOSTLE

How can you spot modern-day Judases? Unfortunately, they do resemble true apostles to a great degree. Satan has cunningly formed these impostors into near look-alikes. Like any counterfeit, if we know what to look for, they can be detected. False apostles are always marked by *false personalities, false practices* and *false proclamations*.

False Personality

When God calls someone to ministry, He begins a process of transformation within that person's character and heart (see Rom. 8:29,30; 12:2; 2 Cor. 3:18). The dealings of God begin deep inside the individual to conform that person to Christ in personality and character. The end result is that the person will possess the internal makeup of a servant of God.

False apostles lack this internal makeup and personality that is present in true apostles. This is because they have not been transformed by the power of Christ from their old natures. Paul says that although they appear to be transformed, it is only because they have transformed *themselves* (just as Satan does), fashioning *themselves* into apostles (see 2 Cor. 11:13-15). They call themselves and develop themselves. They have no true sanctification or character development process within themselves. They are not, nor ever appear, completely changed by God.

This lack of internal transformation by God's power can ultimately be detected on two levels.

First, these men will possess no intimacy of relationship with Christ; they are not abiding in the vine. To such counterfeits Christ Himself will proclaim on judgment day, "I never knew you; depart from Me, you who practice lawlessness!" (Matt. 7:23).

Second, false apostles will have no real relationship or fellowship with true believers. The New Testament speaks of false ministers as being "false brethren" (2 Cor. 11:26; Gal. 2:4,5). This phrase points to the question of their relationship and identity within the Body of Christ. They are not "brethren," and have no place of relationship among the brethren or in the Father's house. These are people that by makeup and relationship stand apart from the true people of God.

False Practices

False apostles can also be detected by how their conduct. Paul spoke of their "cunning craftiness"—false methods that reveal their false identities (see Eph. 4:14). Their false practices are extensions of their false characters. Scripture reveals many practices that characterize false apostles, including the presence of the following elements:

- *Secrecy and mystery in their doctrines and lives instead of openness* (see Gal. 2:4,5). "Keeping secrets" is a good indication that something is wrong.
- *A Spirit of bondage or control of others instead of promoting true liberty* (see 2:4,5). A true apostle never wants to bind or control anyone. (For more information about how true apostles use their authority, see chapter 11).
- *Manipulation through flattering words instead of speaking the truth in love* (see Rom. 16:18; Eph. 4:15).
- *A sexually-seductive influence of women instead of purity and respect* (see Matt. 23:14; 2 Tim. 3:6).
- *Deception and pretense instead of honesty and integrity* (see Matt. 7:15; 24:11).
- *False miracles born out of a demonic empowerment instead of true miracles by the power of the Holy Spirit* (see 24:24).
- *Superstitions, false philosophies and carnal thinking instead of the mind of Christ and heavenly wisdom* (see Col. 2:8; Jas. 3:15).
- *Empty traditions and lifeless symbolism instead of meaningful worship* (see Col. 2:8,18).
- *Penetrating the local church with their messages instead of penetrating society with the gospel* (see Acts 20:29; Jude 4). True apostles do not come into the local church to draw people to themselves. This is the work of false apostles. True apostles are concerned about winning the lost.
- *Detracting and drawing away from the local church and toward themselves instead of building it up and drawing people to Christ* (see Acts 20:30; 1 John 2:19,26)

Each of these practices are observable and contrary to proper ministry methods. Consistent violations of the principles at stake may be clear indications of a false ministry at work.

False Proclamation

False apostles lack valid apostolic messages. They can never sound right because they are not right. Their teachings are not based on truth, but are rooted in deceptions that are entwined within their false thinking, reaching out to draw others in with dark powers. Whether they "pervert the gospel" (Gal. 1:7) or preach a "different gospel" entirely (2 Cor. 11:4; Gal. 1:6), they receive curses for doing so (see Gal. 1:9). The insidious danger of the messages false ministers propagate is that they are not their own, but are actually "doctrines of demons," issuing from hell itself (1 Tim. 4:1). The grim results of following their teachings manifest in the form of personal heartaches, spiritual turmoil as well as eternal damnation.

In short, false apostles have false personalities, practices and proclamations. They can be known by their fruit, and action should be taken to limit their effectiveness.

FOUR LAWS IN DEALING WITH FALSE APOSTLES

What do you do with a Judas, once he has been detected? The first thing we must evaluate is whether this person is a *false apostle* or a *fallen apostle*. The answer to that question determines the strategy and the desired outcome. In this chapter we are dealing with false apostles, so I'll save my remarks about fallen apostles for the next chapter where I will discuss the apostolic authority and mutual accountability among apostles.

In the case of a false apostle, we must keep in mind that Christ's response to Judas, despite the fact that Jesus knew what Judas was about to do, was not violent or vitriolic. The battle is not against flesh and blood. We are taught in Scripture to respond to false apostles decisively, but spiritually. What laws and principles govern the treatment of false apostles in the Church of Jesus Christ?

1. Avoid Coming Under their Influence

The first law is based on the *principle of prevention*: Through building our knowledge of the Word, we are able to spot false apostles and avoid them before they are able to bring their influence into our lives (see Rom. 16:17; Titus 3:9). We must never, under any circumstances, place ourselves under their leadership or within their sphere of influence, even briefly: "And this occurred because of false brethren secretly brought in (who came in by stealth to spy out our liberty which we have in Christ Jesus, that they might bring us into bondage), *to whom we did not yield submission even for an hour,* that the truth of the gospel might continue with you" (Gal. 2:4,5, emphasis mine).

2. Abandon All Connections with Them

Totally separate and withdraw yourself from false apostles. This law is based on the *principle of preservation:* "Do not be deceived: 'Bad company ruins good morals'" (1 Cor. 15:33, NRSV). True apostles cannot afford to associate themselves with men of spurious character, even in the interest of unity, networking or fellowship (see Gal. 5:12; 2 Thess. 3:6,14; 2 John 1:6). Paul warned Timothy that such are "men of corrupt minds and destitute of the truth, who suppose that godliness is a means of gain. From such withdraw yourself" (1 Tim. 6:5). Whether we are apostles or apostolic people, we need to distance ourselves from Satan's counterfeits. Our motive is not fear, it is prudence. The apostolic movement can be contaminated quickly if this principle is not observed.

3. Admonish and Exhort Them to Cease from Their False Practices

False apostles must be challenged by godly men. This law draws its force from the *principle of purification:* The only way to keep the Body of Christ free from impurity is to confront it. Scripture calls the person of God to exhort and convince false ministries, "Holding fast the faithful word as he has been taught, that he may be able, by sound doctrine, both to exhort and convict those who contradict" (Titus 1:9). This approach is to be repeated up to two times, after which the false minister who continues to practice deception should be marked and rejected from fellowship and association because of self-condemnation (see Titus 3:10,11).

4. Alert Others in the Body of Christ of Their Works

This law rests upon the *principle of protection:* We must guard the Body of Christ from infections that will weaken or defile it. A substantial portion of the New Testament consists of apostles identifying spiritual dangers and alerting the Body not to approach them. It is proper to specifically identify wrongdoers (see Rom. 16:17). This protects the house of God from unwanted invasions, and ensures the health of the Body.

SUMMARY

Scripture is clear that apostolic ministry will be targeted by Satan for neutralization. The true apostles who are anointed and appointed for the final hour of world harvest will constitute such a threat to the demonic kingdom that a massive countermovement will arise in retaliation. A company of false apostles will arise concurrent with the company of the true. The aim of this demonic assault will be to weaken the apostolic movement and detract from its effect on earth.

That the enemy will be defeated by the Church is clear; the modern movement of Judas Iscariots will hang themselves and ultimately fall, while the true company of apostles will move forward to receive power and claim the nations. The victory can come only as God's people are able to discern between true and false apostles, and will respond by properly *understanding apostolic authority*.

Note
1.   Frank Damazio, *The Vanguard Leader* (Portland, Oreg.: Bible Temple, 1994), p. 161.

UNDERSTANDING APOSTOLIC AUTHORITY

IT WAS A LESSON THEY WOULD NEVER FORGET. IT STARTED WITH WHAT seemed to be an innocent request. They felt a little strange about it, but, after all, they were apostles. They had been personally selected to follow Christ and be with Him. Surely Jesus would understand and grant their requests. So they decided to ask.

"Master, we want you to grant us our special requests," John carefully appealed.

"What would you like?" queried Christ with a curious smile.

James explained: "We'd like to each have a special place at Your side in glory...when Your kingdom is...."

"You don't know what you are asking," Christ interjected. His face grew serious. "Can you drink of the cup that I drink of? And can you be baptized with the baptism that I am baptized with?"

Undaunted, they both answered, "We can."

Jesus brought the discussion to a new level of prophetic intensity. "You will truly drink of the cup that I drink of, and you shall experience the same baptism. But what you are asking is not mine to decide. Those positions will be given to those for whom they have been prepared."

The two began to flush red with embarrassment. They had revealed their own petty ambitions. The other apostles had become aware of the conversation and the atmosphere was turning quickly against them. Worse yet, Jesus had shown His clear displeasure for their requests.

The Lord diffused the tension by steering them into a detailed discourse concerning the nature of ministry. They needed to understand something, and Christ almost always used occasions when the apostles had made mistakes as opportunities to correct and teach them. They needed to understand apostolic authority.

He went on to contrast authority in the Kingdom with authority in the world; they were not the same. Greatness in the Kingdom was a result of sincere servitude, not carnal competition. Pointing to Himself as a pattern, Christ revealed that although He was Lord of all, He came to serve and not to be served (see Matt. 20:20-28; Mark 10:35-45).

Ever since James and John made that selfish request for position, the issue of the scope of the apostle's authority has been contemplated. Certainly apostles are called to exercise authority, but Christ had made it clear that this authority was to be earned humbly, motivated properly and rewarded sovereignly.

To this issue we now direct our efforts to understand the ministry of the apostle. How much authority do apostles have? How much should they use? Are there lines of authority for apostles, and how are they structured? Understanding the implications of the patterns of New Testament apostolic authority for today is essential to the success of the coming apostolic movement and the development of the apostolic individual.

EARLY PATTERNS OF APOSTOLIC AUTHORITY

As we have seen, the twelve apostles struggled as men to understand the limits and nature of their calling. In their early days as apostles, their hearts had been troubled at the prospect of Christ's departure (see John 14:1,27). This was likely true for a number of reasons, not the least of which may have been the issue of who would assume oversight of the Twelve. It is likely that Peter's leadership among the Twelve was tested from time to time, especially when he made the mistakes he is so well remembered for today. Though the listings of the names of the apostles in the Gospels always place Peter first in order, it is clear that not everyone was satisfied with his preeminence (see Mark 9:34; Luke 22:24).

When Jesus was physically present and in charge of the Twelve, most of the hidden positioning and competition was held in check. But when Christ ascended to the Father, a vacuum was created. Someone needed to fill His slot. We have no record of Christ officially appointing Peter as the new head of the Kingdom effort,[1] and an uncertainty of Peter's authority may have prevailed.

As time unfolded, Peter did become the unofficial leader of the Church. After the Resurrection and Christ's effort to encourage the disciple who denied Him, it was clear that Jesus still had something great in mind for Peter. By the Day of Pentecost, he had become a greatly transformed man, and was used mightily by God to provide insight and leadership on that eventful day. He is mentioned by the writer of Acts as appearing first and speaking first (see Acts 1:15; 2:14; 3:12). From that time on, Peter figures into the early chapters of Acts as a forerunner and a representative of the apostles, receiving honor as first among them whenever they are referred to as a group (see 2:39; 5:29).

As the narrative of Acts further unfolds, Luke's attention shifts to other apostles. Peter's prominence among the Jews pales as Paul's conversion and ministry to the Gentiles expands. Paul then becomes the central apostolic figure in Acts, implying that his presence even overshadowed that of Peter. We know that early in Paul's apostleship, he was comfortable enough with his authority to publicly correct Peter for his apparent religious prejudice (see Gal. 2:11-14). By the time we get to Acts 15, and the apostolic council that was convened to address the problem of circumcision of the Gentiles, the apostle James had replaced Peter as the leading apostle and authority in Jerusalem.

So within the first few decades after the Resurrection, the Church's leadership shifted several times among apostolic figures. Each one was raised up by God for a particular season of influence and purpose. Their places of authority were not unchangeable. They were built upon their foundational callings as apostles, but were relative to the seasons and purposes of God for their lives and for the Church.

This type of flexibility within the leadership of the apostles powerfully demonstrates that apostolic authority is neither *successional* (that is, able to be permanently imparted at the will of man) nor *hierarchical* (composed of numerous layers of authority) in its basic nature. Instead, leadership and submission among apostles is fluid, relational and subject to change as the situation and the will of God may dictate. This fact provides for us an important introduction to the first of four spiritual principles that influenced apostolic authority structures in the Early Church. First, let's examine the source of all spiritual authority—a servant's heart.

The Source of Apostolic Authority

The apostle is first and foremost a servant. All true ministry is a result of a heartfelt commitment to humbly lay aside one's own agenda and serve the Father. This is the example set by Christ—the Apostle—Who came not to be served, but to serve (see Matt. 20:28). An apostle received the revelation of the power of Christ's greatness through servitude:

> Let this mind be in you which was also in Christ Jesus, who, being in the form of God, did not consider it robbery to be equal with God, but made Himself of no reputation, taking the form of a bondservant, and coming in the likeness of men. And being found in appearance as a man, He humbled Himself and became obedient to the point of death, even the death of the cross. Therefore God also has highly exalted Him and given Him the name which is above every name, that at the name of Jesus every knee should bow (Phil. 2:5-10).

These powerful words contain a revelation and wisdom that is eternal. An apostle's greatness and authority come from serving. Those who desire an authoritative apostolic ministry must be prepared to take on the form of a servant and experience the cross, so a glorious resurrection of greater authority can be birthed into their lives.

Reflections of Apostolic Humility

Paul described his ministry for the Lord as characterized by "all humility of mind" (Acts 20:19, *KJV*). The quality of humility and the servant's attitude were deeply rooted in his inner man. Consider three reflections of this kind of apostolic humility in the New Testament mirror:

1. The Apostles Saw Themselves as Slaves of Jesus Christ

The apostles identified themselves in their writings as servants. For example: "Paul, a bondservant of Jesus Christ, called to be an apostle, separated to the gospel of God" (Rom. 1:1). This was not just a trademark of Paul's letters, but similar introductions are to be found in the writings of the apostles James (see Jas. 1:1), Peter (see 2 Pet. 1:1) and John (see Rev. 1:1).

The apostles were communicating that they understood their roles. They were subservient to Christ. They found their purposes and identities in lifestyles of doing the will of God, yielding all their abilities. As bond slaves, their rights and privileges were forfeited, and the responsibilities assigned to them by Christ took preeminence.

2. The Apostles Never Took Glory for Themselves

The humility of mind that is characteristic of apostles prevents them from drawing attention to themselves. The apostle Paul confessed, "if I preach the gospel, I have nothing to boast of, for necessity is laid upon me; yes, woe is me if I do not preach the gospel!" (1 Cor. 9:16). One of the most accomplished and supernatural men of all time sincerely believed he had no reason to boast. This is typical of the humility empowering an apostle.

Whenever God used the apostles to demonstrate supernatural healing power, they were careful to give God the glory. Evidently some were attributing this power to them, but the apostles demonstrated a rare humility and said, "why look so intently at us, as though by our own power or godliness we had made this man walk?"(Acts 3:12).

Later on, when Peter came to the home of Cornelius, we read that as he came in, "Cornelius met him and fell down at his feet and worshiped him. But Peter lifted him up, saying, 'Stand up; I myself am also a man'" (Acts 10:25,26). Apostles are aware of their frail humanity (see Acts 14:11-15) and are not given to self glory (see 1 Thess. 2:6).

It should be noted, however, that the qualities of humility and servitude did not keep the apostles from demonstrating fierce boldness (see Acts 13:46; 14:3). The apostles bravely encountered disease, opposition, persecution and natural hardships. It has been rightly said that meekness does not mean weakness, and in the case of the apostles, their frail humility never prevented them from confrontation and conquest.

3. The Apostles Understood Their Own Need to Submit

Far from being individuals who view themselves as a "law unto themselves," true apostles manifest their humility through a tangible submission to proper authority. The apostles Paul and Barnabas did not leave the church at Antioch until they were properly sent by the Holy Spirit through the local leadership (see Acts 13:1-3). In this context, we witness the apostles' submission *to the sending church*. This humble subordination appears to have been perpetual, for a quick review of the apostolic journeys of Paul reveals that he always began each trip at Antioch, and returned to Antioch to report his progress at the end (e.g., Acts 14:26-28).

It is also clear from the same Scriptures that the apostles understood their need to submit to the authority of those who were overseeing local churches that they themselves did not found. They understood *submission to the local church.* Neither Paul nor Barnabas founded Antioch, and when they were present there, they never sought to rule the roost. In fact, we have no record of apostles ever usurping authority in *any* ministry context.

It appears that the apostles in the New Testament knew how to "behave as guests in another man's house," never making unwelcome attempts at controlling another man's work. As a further example, when Paul strongly desired Apollos to come to Corinth, and Apollos was not willing to do so in the time frame that Paul desired, Paul accepted it gracefully and refrained from trying to manipulate him into compliance (see 1 Cor. 16:12). Whether it is in relation to a sending church or another ministry, we always detect the quiet heartbeat of humble submission constantly beating in the true apostle's breast.

FOUR PRINCIPLES OF APOSTOLIC AUTHORITY

What can be learned from the New Testament about the philosophy of leadership that guided the apostles through those exciting early decades? How can we adapt these timeless principles in the present apostolic move? The following four principles of apostolic authority lend insight:

1. The Principle of Interdependent Cooperation

It has already been stated that the apostle's heart was truly humble.

Apostles never saw themselves as men who controlled the lives of those submitted to them, but respected man's free will and chose cooperation instead of control.

Throughout the New Testament this principle holds true. Wherever people and leaders exist, there must be cooperation instead of domination. In Revelation 2, the Lord Jesus indicates His hatred of both the deeds and the doctrines of the Nicolaitans (see Rev. 2:6,15). Though not much is known of this sect, we can glean insight into its errors from its name. The Greek root *nikao* means "to conquer," and the root *laos* means "people," hence the Nicolaitans were *people conquerors*—those who dominated and controlled the saints. True apostles would never be guilty of such control.

Paul revealed this when he wrote to the Corinthian believers, saying: "Not that we have dominion over your faith, but are fellow workers for your joy; for by faith you stand" (2 Cor. 1:24). Paul understood that the saints at Corinth, though they needed correction and disciplined change, were not to be placed in a position of dependence upon his faith. They needed to stand on their own faith. Paul's role was to help them walk in joy instead of defeat. Neither were they to become recklessly *independent* of his apostolic authority. This popular attitude leaves the believer cut off from a great deal of blessing released through relationship with leadership. Instead, they were to maintain the principle of *interdependence in the local church:* the intricate interlacing of apostolic leadership, local leadership (such as pastors and elders) and the local membership in harmony and balance. Neither the apostle, the local leadership nor the people can be complete without the other.

This balanced connection would become God's means of growth and strength for the Church, not only in the first century, but in our own as well. The present apostolic move must be baptized in a sensitivity to the complete interdependent relationships God has designed to work within His people (see Eph. 4:16; Phil. 2:2).

2. The Principle of Voluntary Submission

When people and their apostles are in proper relationship to each other, both genuine respect and true submission are present. Apostles such as Paul regularly exercised influence over believers and churches in their roles as leaders and spiritual fathers. For example, the people obeyed the decisions reached by the elders and apostles at Jerusalem. "And as they went through the cities, they delivered to them the decrees to keep, which were determined by the apostles and elders at Jerusalem. So the churches were strengthened in faith, and increased in number daily" (Acts 16:4,5).

Was this excessive control? Definitely not. These verses indicate that the people actually prospered as they obeyed. This blessing came because the principle of voluntary submission was in operation. Relational submission is voluntary. Paul points this out when speaking of false ministers: "to whom we did not yield submission even for an hour" (Gal. 2:5). Submission is yielded by an act of the will.

The apostles could not demand submission and cooperation from the people, but they could receive it from them when it was willingly extended. As the people voluntarily submitted, the apostles led and governed. This is the true pattern for submission and godly authority in the home, the church and the government. A leader cannot lead unless people willingly follow, nor can an apostle demand a response because he is an apostle. Apostles are servants who minister to those who will freely receive their authority.

Along these lines, some have asked, "If we are coming into a new dimension of church government because of the emergence of apostles and the apostolic movement, what will this mean for the current structures in the Church such as denominations? Will we abandon them wholesale to join the organizations headed by the new breed of apostles?" Although I cannot claim to have the complete answer to this important question, I do believe that whatever rearranging God does in His church will not violate the biblical principles of authority I am presenting in this chapter. In other words, I do not believe we will have a giant mess on our hands. Unity will develop as God helps us to interdependently cooperate and voluntarily submit to one another. This movement should not produce a violation of the principles of apostolic authority, but rather a fulfillment of them for a greater unity between the many diverse camps in the Body of Christ. I do not know exactly how we are going to get there, but I know that we shall, for Jesus has asked the Father to perform it (see John 17:20-23).

3. The Principle of Local Autonomy

When we examine patterns of authority in the New Testament, clearly several levels of authority existed. There was of course, the local level of authority that flowed within the local church. In this setting, pastors and elders governed the work of God and administrated the completion of the purposes of the gospel within their church assembly. Beyond local authority was the translocal authority of the apostles who normally oversaw the work of God within a particular sphere of either geographical or cultural influence.

As we examine the interrelationships of local and translocal authority in Scripture, we find a wonderful balance. Apostles worked carefully with local churches and their leaderships, especially within churches they planted. In Acts 15 and 16 alone, the apostles worked hand-in-glove with the local leaders in a variety of functions. Paul and Barnabas held dialogues with the other apostles and leaders in Jerusalem about the problem of the circumcision of the Gentiles (see Acts 15:2,6). As apostles, Paul and Barnabas were received by the apostles and leaders in Jerusalem (see v. 4). They were then sent by the apostles and leaders of Jerusalem, accompanied by letters and other men, to go to Antioch and convey the findings of the apostolic council (see v. 22). As has been previously noted, the apostles and local leaders also stood together and issued an authoritative decree for the whole Gentile church to observe and follow.

In all of this cooperation, the apostles' translocal authority never overrode local authority. The principle of local autonomy and self-rule remained constant, while the authority of the apostles in council together was governing the broader scope of the work of God.

4. The Principle of Mutual Accountability

Wherever authority exists, the potential for abuse of that authority is present. God has designed authority structures whereby lower levels of authority become accountable to higher levels. For example, in an army, foot soldiers are authorized to make war, but are accountable to sergeants, who are accountable to captains, who are accountable to generals. These generals are accountable to heads of state.

In the army of God, this holds true as well, but who keeps the generals (for our purposes, the apostles and fathers of the Church) accountable besides God Himself?

What we observe in the New Testament is this principle of mutual accountability wherein the "generals" become accountable *to one anoth-*

er. This principle mandates that people become accountable to their top-level peers as well as to their ultimate head. It creates an effective relational network whereby authorities (especially in positions of headship) maintain openness, communication and teachability with one another. Within this arrangement, submission to one another is practiced and abuses are avoided.

This raises the question of *fallen apostles,* which we mentioned in the last chapter. What should be done with an apostle who sins or gets off track? The kind of relational accountability I am describing is the best prevention I know of for such a problem, however in the instance where a sinning brother must be dealt with, his peers need to restore him with wisdom, sensitivity to timing and a careful self-examination (see Gal. 6:1,2). The loving confrontation and correction of peers can provide a safety net that is needed in apostolic ministry. In the event that the sinning brother is not repentant, harsher methods would need to be employed (see Titus 3:10,11). In either case, true accountability, if exercised properly, provides protection from error and recourse when errors are made.

In the apostolic council of Acts 15, the apostles came together in this spirit of mutual accountability to settle disputes and doctrinal problems. They gathered regularly and submitted to the admonition and counsel of one another. Some had to change and conform to the decisions agreed upon by apostolic peers. This is mutual accountability in action. Along these lines, Paul's open rebuke of Peter in Galatians 2 reveals that apostles were free, if not obligated, to chasten each other for any wrongdoing.

FOUR ASPECTS OF APOSTOLIC AUTHORITY

What other factors need to be considered in understanding apostolic authority? Consider these additional facets of the discussion:

1. Ranks of Apostleship

It is entirely possible that an informal ranking structure existed among the apostles of the first century. We observe many indications that this was likely. First, James was preeminent in his position at Jerusalem's council meeting. His character, gifting and influence as the leader of the first church made him a natural leader of apostles. Second, Paul's language indicates the presence of "super apostles" or chief apostles (see 2 Cor. 11:5; 12:11), as well as lesser apostles (see 1 Cor. 15:9). These phrases prompt us to identify informal levels of ministry among apostles such as we would see in any organization today.

2. Reach of Authority

Second Corinthians 10:13-16 indicates that each apostle is given a unique measure of rule (or sphere of authority) by God. It was important that each apostle understand this, and not exceed the appointed limits of ministry. Both natural and spiritual reasons for this kind of awareness and limitation are clearly delineated among the apostles of the New Testament. For example, Paul's sphere of ministry was the Gentile world (see Rom. 11:13); Peter's was to the Jewish world (see Gal. 2:8), as was James and John's (see Gal. 2:7-10). It is interesting to consider the appointment of Matthias as the replacement of Judas in this light. Each apostle's role is precise and necessary in the broad balance of apostolic authority.

3. Relational Authority

Dick Iverson wisely observes, "Relationship, not hierarchy, is the basis of spiritual authority. Holding a position, filling an office, or being elected to a place of importance is not how spiritual elders are made— they earn it! One qualifies to be a leader by developing relationships."[2]

For this reason, we should also be aware that apostles are apostles to some, and not to others. Just as in the Church today people relate to "their pastors" differently than they do to another's, in the Early Church a sense of identification with a specific apostle was based on personal relationship. Epaphroditus was known as *"your messenger"* (literally, "your apostle"). To some he was a relational overseer, and by implication, to others he was not. Because Paul was not in authority over Jerusalem, he submitted to James while there. This relational aspect of the apostle's authority is no doubt what Paul had in mind when he said, "If I am not an apostle to others, yet doubtless I am to you. For you are the seal of my apostleship in the Lord" (1 Cor. 9:2).

4. Regional Authority

The sphere of authority in combination with relational authority may lead us to another aspect of the apostle's authority—that of *regional* or *territorial apostleship*. Roland Allen suggests that the apostles targeted entire regions when he wrote, "Both St. Luke and St. Paul speak constantly of the provinces rather than of the cities. Thus St. Paul was forbidden to preach the word in Asia; he was called from Troas not to Philippi or to Thessalonica, but to Macedonia. Speaking of the collection for the saints at Jerusalem, St. Paul says that he boasted that Achaia was ready a year ago. The suggestion is that in St. Paul's view the unit was the province rather than the city."[3] We believe that the Holy Spirit works among apostles to divide regions among them so that geographical areas (such as continents) can be uniformly penetrated. This kind of a division of responsibility and effort is in keeping with the prudent nature of God.

Scripture indicates that the apostles migrated to specific territories in their activities. Paul's ministry took him to Palestine, Syria, Cyprus, Asia Minor, Macedonia, Greece and Rome. Illyricum and Spain are also mentioned (see Rom. 15:19-24). Many interpret 1 Peter 5:13 to mean that Peter traveled to Babylon, or modern Iraq. Tradition has it that Thomas went to India, and others went to France, Britain and northern Europe.

It is fascinating to consider the remarks of J. Danielou as quoted by Dr. McBirnie: "At the beginning of Book III of his History of the Church, after having described the Fall of Jerusalem, Eusebius says that 'the inhabited world' was divided into zones of influence among the Apostles: Thomas in the region of the Parthians, John in Asia, Peter in Pontus and Rome, Andrew in Scythia (*The Christian Centuries*, J. Danielou, p. 39)."[4]

Later on in history, St. Augustine of Canterbury was known as "the apostle to England" and St. Patrick as "the apostle to Ireland." Apostles have historically been burdened for specific territories of the earth. If Satan has established territorial spirits to run the global battle against the Church, as many today believe, is it not possible that God also has established territorial apostles to help counteract their destructive activity? The dynamics for world evangelization that become possible when apostles properly relate to one another in all these aspects is thrilling.

APOSTOLIC FUNCTIONS
RELATIVE TO AUTHORITY

An in-depth study of the apostle's ministry would not be complete without considering apostolic functions relative to authority. The spiritual authority delegated to apostles mandates the administration of the following responsibilities:

Apostles Ordain Order (1 Cor. 7:17; 11:34; 16:1)

The apostle Paul was proactive in overseeing the believer's lifestyle, methods of giving and general conduct. His sphere of influence brought order and excellence to the house of God. Clearly, apostles have been given real authority to govern and influence everything from doctrinal questions to the practical issues of living for God. The New Testament letters bear evidence to this aspect of apostleship.

Apostles Settle Doctrinal Questions (Acts 15:1,2,6)

The apostles convened in Jerusalem out of need for doctrinal clarity. Apostles today could function similarly to establish doctrinal harmony in God's Word and unity among themselves. I'm not sure how far this harmony will go, but I see an encouraging openness among various theological camps today that I hope will be aided by the emergence of apostles. This would doubtless contribute to the "unity of the faith" Paul spoke of as being so vital in the Church (see Eph. 4:13).

Apostles Make Decrees (Acts 16:4)

Once the apostles and elders had reached a consensus in Jerusalem, they sent out decrees. These are specific ordinances (literally dogmas) relative to the Church and its members. If apostles ordain order, this order is communicated through the use of decrees.

We also see decrees working on a smaller scale. For example, in the apostolic network of which I am a part, problems sometimes arise in churches concerning issues such as money, decisions or doctrine. When an impasse occurs that the local church cannot resolve on its own, our network will send an apostle who will make a binding decision or decree after a full hearing about the matter. Everyone involved is obliged to flow with this decision so that progress in the church can continue. In either case, it is clear that in ministry, decisions often need to be made, and sometimes the apostles must make them.

Apostles Set Deacons and Elders into Their Offices (Acts 6:1-4,6; 14:23)

Scripture views ordination for ministry as of utmost importance.

Apostles initiated such occasions and were on hand for them, possessing the authority from God to impart release for service and recognition by God to the lives of those specially selected.

Apostles Delegated Authority to "Subapostolic" Leaders

The nature of apostolic ministry necessitated local overseers (such as pastors and elders) to be placed in charge of the work of God. The apostle Paul ordained one such overseer named Timothy, and apparently Paul charged him with the oversight of several churches. Many believe that these men were recognized by the title "bishop" for their oversight of multiple congregations. Evidently such responsibility was a perfect source of training for men as they became apostles—as Timothy later did.

As the Church approaches the apostolic dimension, we must investigate the principles that guided the apostles of the first century replicated in our century. We must be willing as a movement to practice the principles of *interdependent cooperation, voluntary submission, local autonomy* and *mutual accountability*. Entire apostolic households must cooperate with their apostolic fathers in a balanced and scriptural way.

Summary

Wherever authority is in place, people must submit to each other in a spirit of love and unity (see Eph. 5:21). The local church must remain strong and independent, yet totally open to the guidance and influence of the apostle. And the fathers must gather together in true relationship and openness, holding one another accountable to the Word and Spirit of Christ for the good of His people. As this is accomplished, the work of God will advance among the nations in a balanced and safe manner, and unity will spread among leaders of diverse backgrounds and perspectives.

Since that fateful day when two young apostles approached Jesus with their request for position and authority, the role of the apostle relative to authority has been explored, clarified and practiced. These two men learned about spiritual authority, but went on to discover spiritual power. As the Church moves forward, we will need to heed the same lessons so that we too can advance and experience *supernatural power*.

Notes

1. The author acknowledges that Roman Catholic church tradition teaches that Matthew 16:18 was Christ's official appointment of Peter as the Church's leading apostle, eventually recognized by them as the first pope. Protestants, however, have not accepted this viewpoint, seeing instead Peter's affirmation of faith (Matt. 16:16) as the "rock" upon whom Christ would build His Church.
2. Christian Equippers International, *The Master Builder* (1985): 147.
3. Roland Allen, *Missionary Methods, St. Paul's or Ours?* (Grand Rapids: Eerdmans, 1962), p. 12.
4. William Steuart McBirnie, *The Search for the Twelve Apostles* (Wheaton, Ill.: 1978), p. 43.

APOSTLES AND
SUPERNATURAL
POWER

IN THE LAST CHAPTER I DISCUSSED THE SUBJECT OF APOSTOLIC AUTHORITY; now we turn our attention to apostolic power. If authority can be understood as the *right* to act, power can be seen as the *ability* to act. For apostles, both are important. One element without the other is incomplete: Possessing spiritual power outside the confines of God's authority has occult overtones, and authority without power is inadequate to address the forces that oppose the work of God. We must look to this important balance of power and authority as the Church embraces the apostolic movement.

The demonstration of true supernatural power is one of the most exciting aspects of the ministry of the apostle and the entire apostolic movement. God's promise to restore all things before the return of Christ surely includes restoring this ingredient to the whole Church in all its fullness (see Acts 3:19-21).

Certainly, apostles are not the only ministries God has called to be supernatural. Still, as I read through the book of Acts, I am struck with the frequency and magnitude of the miracles and demonstrations of God's power through the lives of the apostles Peter, John and Paul. God's power was a continual experience for them. "And through the hands of the apostles many signs and wonders were done among the people" (Acts 5:12). One gets the sense that proper apostolic ministry cannot be separated from the miraculous power of God. We are approaching a time when we will see the fullness of God's supernatural power gloriously manifested in apostles and in the entire Body of Christ.

POWER NEEDED, POWER PROMISED

Jesus told the apostles about a spiritual power that would be imparted, and it would drive the evangelization of the world. Acts 1:8 states: "But you shall receive power when the Holy Spirit has come upon you; and you shall be witnesses to Me in Jerusalem, and in all Judea and Samaria, and to the end of the earth." Such power would be imperative in the face of such an awesome task. Indeed, these words were fulfilled in the lives of those great apostles to whom Christ spoke.

The power of the Holy Spirit will be the current that gives the emerging apostolic movement its intensity. As in the first apostolic wave, this present wave will rise up in obedience to the command of the Spirit of God. This power should be evident in the lives of present-day apostles. Although having a miracle ministry is not proof that a person is an apostle, nowhere in Scripture is apostolic ministry endorsed as anything less than supernatural. We have already seen that after patience, signs, wonders and mighty deeds are the authenticating marks on the touchstone of apostleship (see 2 Cor. 12:12). The idea of apostles without supernatural anointing falls short of the picture of apostolic ministry painted in the New Testament.

MODERN POWER FAILURES

Those who oppose charismatic gifts and the miracle power of the Spirit will doubtless take exception to this point. At present, a regrettable trend is occurring in the Body of Christ to polarize about the issue of supernatural power of God. Opponents of the ministry of the Spirit seem to recognize that the apostolic office carries with it the demonstration of the power of God. They appear to assert that signs and wonders ceased at the death of the first-century apostles, and because there are no longer any apostles in the Body of Christ, any supernatural operation is suspect. This view leaves the Church in a dead stall, unable to move forward in supernatural power.

We who identify both with the present-day ministry of apostles and with signs and wonders have several sound reasons for believing as we do. Although the purpose of this work is less concerned with convincing critics than inspiring believers, a brief summary may be helpful.

THE HEART OF GOD

Signs and wonders provide a powerful expression of God's love for people. Throughout Scripture, we see God enabling His servants to perform miraculous works so that His people would be healed, delivered and encouraged. This flow of supernatural power always issues from the love of God. In the Old Testament (a covenant inferior to the New), Moses employed miracles in delivering Israel from Egyptian bondage. God heard their groaning and was moved with compassion to deliver them with power (see Exod. 2:23-25). The prophet Elijah demonstrated God's heart of compassion when God raised a widow's son from the dead through the miracle power of God (see 1 Kings 17:21-24). Dozens of other miracles and signs occurred.

In the New Testament, Jesus Christ demonstrated God's heart daily through healings, resurrections, deliverances and providing for the needy. What's more, He clearly instructed the apostles to do the same. What is the Bible if it is not the record of God's supernatural power flowing through His people to demonstrate His nature of love and compassion? Nothing has changed in the character of God: He is still compassionate, loving and generous, and He still heals, delivers and provides through supernatural power for His chosen servants.

How tragic that the Church has operated for so long with so little miraculous power. Like the apostles in the early part of their ministries, we have been given authority, but we have lacked power. Though Jesus gave the Twelve all authority (see Mark 6:7), the apostles at one point were unable to cast out a demonic spirit that was woefully oppressing a young boy. Though they had the spiritual *authority*, they lacked the spiritual *power*. When the father of the child approached Jesus and reported the apostles' failure, Jesus sharply corrected them for lack of faith, and proceeded to deliver the boy Himself (see Mark 9:14-29).

Truly the world is waiting for the Church to rise with this kind of power to address its oppressions. I am convinced that as the world is drawn toward more and more occult powers and experiences, people will not give ear to a powerless Church. It is certain that the same Jesus who corrected and instructed His disciples on that day wants us to obtain the necessary power for delivering the captive and healing the sick.

Gloriously, God is revealing spiritual power through His people in our day. We are beginning to understand our authority and the power of faith. We are beginning to tap into the hidden resources of prayer and fasting. The need for compassion and intercession is being unearthed by those who search for spiritual power in their ministries. Although a few are experiencing this dimension of God in its fullness, people by the millions have tasted of the firstfruits of the greater anointing God has promised to pour out in the last days. As we absorb these truths and anointings, God is beginning to restore the Apostolic Spirit to the Body of Christ.

POWER FROM INTIMACY

Before looking at the kinds of power in which apostles operate, we must consider where this power originates. Clearly, supernatural power, which comes from God through the Holy Spirit, indwells the believer. How is that power made operative in ministry?

The apostles of the New Testament experienced the power of God in their lives because they were intimate with God. They were constantly involved in prayer and worship. They prayed in the Upper Room (see Acts 1:14) and in the Temple (see 3:1). They prayed in the midst of persecution, asking for great boldness (see 4:24-30). They prayed about the ordination of deacons and elders (see 6:6; 14:23). They gathered at Antioch for extended periods of time, ministering to the Lord (see 13:1-3). They praised God at the worst moments of their lives (see 16:25). They made a priority of spending time developing this intimacy, saying to all, "We will give ourselves continually to prayer and to the ministry of the word" (6:4).

This kind of intimacy with God permeated their ministries with a tangible anointing. People were able to see the love and power of Jesus shining through them. As they preached, their faces reflected a power that issued from the presence of God: "Now when they saw the boldness of Peter and John,...they marveled. And they realized that they had been with Jesus" (4:13). Being in the presence of Jesus was the key to the power the apostles experienced.

Apostles have been given no other source of power than the power that comes through intimacy with Christ. Cindy Jacobs foresees an increasing blend of the apostolic and intercessory giftings in our decade, presumably meaning that the apostolic movement and the worldwide prayer movement will synergize.[1] This is essential to the apostolic movement because of the elevated intimacy with God that will result. The keys to power in the emerging apostolic movement will be prayer, praise and worship—those activities that involve us in His presence. Intimate relationship with Christ is the foundation for modern manifestations of supernatural power.

SEVEN MANIFESTATIONS OF SUPERNATURAL APOSTOLIC POWER

What supernatural powers do apostles demonstrate? In what shape does God's power manifest in the life of an apostle? A survey of the New Testament reveals at least seven supernatural powers in which apostles have moved.

1. Apostles Supernaturally Attract Large Audiences

Many important ministries in the Body of Christ are referred to as the "hidden" ministries because few ever see the work and sacrifice involved in that person's ministry. Intercessors, for example, seldom receive credit for their hours of ministry. These kinds of ministries are essential and honorable in the work of the Kingdom.

The ministry of apostleship, on the other hand, is a very public ministry. Apostles are usually not quiet, and generally do not work behind the scenes. Their roles involve working with large numbers of people—whether the people are saved or unsaved. This is not to say that apostles *continually* attract large audiences, because that would not be true. The fact remains: the supernatural anointing of the apostle, in the right setting, will often attract large groups of people.

At Pentecost, after the outpouring of the Spirit and the apostle Peter's subsequent sermon, a massive group of 3,000 were saved (see Acts 2:41). At Antioch, almost the entire city came to hear the apostles Paul and Barnabas (see 13:44). More than two dozen times in Acts,

Luke refers to a multitude gathering in connection with the ministry of an apostle.

In the vast majority of cases where multitudes gathered before apostles, it was because of a demonstration of supernatural power. Simply put: *miracles attract multitudes*. There is nothing like a demonstration of divine power to pull otherwise disinterested people together for a presentation of the gospel. What a tool this was for the apostle! It is one that is needed in ministry today. It is no wonder Luke recorded, "With great power the apostles gave witness to the resurrection of the Lord Jesus. And great grace was upon them all" (4:33).

2. God Uses Apostles to Supernaturally Impart Through the Laying on of Hands

Beyond their ability to attract large audiences of the unsaved, apostles are revealed in the New Testament as men who laid their hands on people for supernatural results. Paul strongly desired to visit the church at Rome saying, "I long to see you, that I may impart to you some spiritual gift, so that you may be established" (Rom. 1:11). The book of Acts records three significant examples of this.

In Acts 8, after Philip's Samaritan outreach produced several converts, the apostles Peter and John laid their hands on them and imparted the gift of the Holy Spirit. This power was so impressive to the recently converted Simon that he attempted to purchase it and met a strong rebuke by Peter! In Acts 19, the apostle Paul laid his hands on the twelve disciples at Ephesus and they spoke in tongues and moved in the spirit of prophecy. The supernatural impartation of the Holy Spirit and an actual activation of the prophecy came through the laying on of the apostles' hands. In Acts 28, Paul's hands were laid on the father of Publius on the island of Melita and his fever and bloody flux were broken. Many conversions to Christ followed this transference of supernatural power and, of course, the apostles always credited God as the source of the power.

The laying on of hands is prominent throughout the New Testament. It always speaks of the impartation of supernatural power. Jesus often laid His hands on people for blessing and healing (see Luke 4:40; 13:13) and directed His disciples to do so until the Great Commission was completed (see Mark 16:18). The laying on of hands was as foundational a doctrine in the Early Church as was repentance and resurrection (see Heb. 6:1,2). Especially in Paul's writing to

Timothy, the laying on of hands is seen as a means of supernaturally imparting spiritual gifting (see 1 Tim. 4:14; 5:22; 2 Tim. 1:6).

The twentieth century has seen a restoration of the practice of the laying on of hands for blessing, healing, deliverance, ordination and impartation within the Church. It is a needed practice today. As the benefits of this kind of ministry continue to build in God's people, the renewal of the apostle's office will be strengthened and the supernatural aspects of ministry will increase.

3. Apostles Possess a Supernatural Spirit of Revelation

Apostles in Scripture also experienced the supernatural manifestation of the Spirit of revelation. Along with this power, they received truth from God, delivered it to the saints and taught the saints to experience it for themselves.

Paul spoke candidly about the place and purposes of revelations in his ministry:

> It is not expedient for me doubtless to glory. *I will come to visions and revelations of the Lord.* I knew a man in Christ above fourteen years ago, (whether in the body, I cannot tell; or whether out of the body, I cannot tell: God knoweth;) such an one caught up to the third heaven. And I knew such a man, (whether in the body, or out of the body, I cannot tell: God knoweth;) How that he was caught up into paradise, and heard unspeakable words, which it is not lawful for a man to utter. Of such an one will I glory: yet of myself I will not glory, but in mine infirmities. For though I would desire to glory, I shall not be a fool; for I will say the truth: but now I forbear, lest any man should think of me above that which he seeth me to be, or that he heareth of me. And lest I should be exalted above measure through *the abundance of the revelations*, there was given to me a thorn in the flesh, the messenger of Satan to buffet me, lest I should be exalted above measure (2 Cor. 12:1-7, *KJV*, emphasis mine).

Paul also cites this supernatural flow of knowledge as a source for much of his teaching when he states: "For I received from the Lord that which I also delivered to you" (1 Cor. 11:23).

This revelatory anointing manifested in the lives of the apostles in several ways: visions were experienced by the apostles (see Acts 10:9-22; 18:9,10; 2 Cor. 12:1; the entire book of Revelation). Peter had a *word of knowledge* about Ananias and Sapphira (see Acts 5:3) and another one about three men being downstairs while he rested on the rooftop in Joppa (see 10:19,20). It is clear that many apostles moved in the supernatural prophetic gifts at times as well (see 1 Tim. 1:18; 2 Tim. 1:6).

In this connection it is inspiring to realize that although prophets are responsible for most of the writings of the Old Testament Scriptures, apostles were the vehicles of the Holy Spirit in writing most of the New Testament Scriptures. This is because of their ability to receive revelations from the Spirit of God. This same anointing of revelation helped the apostles interpret and apply the Old Testament Scriptures to contemporary events (see Acts 2:17,25,41; 3:18,22-26; 13:15-23; 15:15ff). The combined effort of the Old Testament prophets and the New Testament apostles to create the written Scriptures (which are the basis for all of our faith and practice) may be what Paul alluded to when he spoke about the Church as being built on the foundation of the apostles and prophets (see Eph. 2:20). Certainly apostles and prophets are both noted for their revelatory abilities (see 3:5).

This experience of receiving revelation was viewed by Paul as desirable for every believer. Ephesians 1:15-23 records a prayer by Paul for the Ephesian believers that they would become filled with *a spirit of revelation*. He taught that believers could receive personal revelations: "How is it then, brethren? when ye come together, *every one of you* hath a psalm, hath a doctrine, hath a tongue, *hath a revelation*, hath an interpretation. *Let all things be done* unto edifying" (1 Cor. 14:26, KJV, emphasis mine).

Paul instructed the believers that some can indeed speak by revelation: "Now, brethren, if I come unto you speaking with tongues, what shall I profit you, except I shall *speak to you either by revelation*, or by knowledge, or by prophesying, or by doctrine?" (1 Cor. 14:6, KJV, emphasis mine)

Whether the apostles were receiving revelation in various ways, communicating what they had received or teaching believers to experience the same thing, one thing is clear. The apostles in the Bible moved in supernatural revelation from the Holy Spirit, and depended upon it for success in ministry. Although the canon of Scripture is unchangeable and complete and today's apostles are not authorized to write their revelations in the form of Scripture, as did their counterparts the prophets, they are nonetheless authorized by pattern and example of the first-century apostles to receive supernatural revelations if they are consistent with Scripture.

4. Apostles Exercise Supernatural Command over Sickness

Scripture reveals a clear pattern of the apostles dealing successfully with sickness and infirmity through spiritual power. This is not surprising, given their example in the great Apostle Jesus, who both modeled His practice and taught them to repeat it. The book of Acts is full of instances in which apostles commanded supernatural power over sickness and achieved astonishing results for the Kingdom.

Peter and John healed a crippled man at the gate Beautiful, and the city of Jerusalem was revolutionized (see Acts 3:1ff). A man who had been bedridden for eight years was instantly healed by Peter in Lydda, and the Bible says that those who dwelt there all turned to the Lord as a result (see 9:32-35). The apostles stayed at Iconium for a season, "speaking boldly in the Lord, who was bearing witness to the word of His grace, granting signs and wonders to be done by their hands" (Acts 14:3). Later on when they came to Lystra, a lame man who had never walked was healed miraculously through a simple command of faith (see vv. 6-10). The locals were so overwhelmed by this demonstration of supernatural power that they attempted to worship Paul and Barnabas as gods. Sometimes unusual miracles were performed through the apostles, such as people being healed by Peter's shadow (see 5:15,16) and from handkerchiefs being sent distances from Paul's body.

What is the value of such displays of God's power? Mainly, to aid the apostles in their tasks of mass evangelization by revealing the love of God in a practical way. As Roland Allen points out, "Miracles were illustrations of the character of the new religion. They were sermons in action. They set forth in unmistakable terms two of its fundamental doctrines, the doctrine of charity and the doctrine of salvation, of release from the bondage of sin and the power of the devil."[2]

Paul and Barnabas were quick to utilize their supernatural power as tools to win people to Christ (see 14:12). In nearly every case in which miracles were performed by the apostles, massive conversions followed. Supernatural power helps to validate and authenticate the ministry of an apostle. Surprisingly, many oppose such power today in the Church. Perhaps if we had this power in more abundant operation we would have the same results the apostles had.

5. Apostles Demonstrate Supernatural Power over Demons

In the book of Acts alone, we find several illuminating instances in which the apostles exercised power to cast out evil spirits:

> Also a multitude gathered from the surrounding cities to Jerusalem, bringing sick people and those who were tormented by *unclean spirits*, and *they were all healed* (5:16, emphasis mine).

> For unclean spirits, crying with a loud voice, came out of many who were *possessed*; and many who were paralyzed and lame were *healed* (8:7, emphasis mine).

> Now it happened, as we went to prayer, that a certain slave girl *possessed with a spirit of divination* met us, who brought her masters much profit by fortune-telling. This girl followed Paul and us, and cried out, saying, "These men are the servants of the Most High God, who proclaim to us the way of salvation." And this she did for many days. But Paul, greatly annoyed, turned and said to the spirit, "I command you in the name of Jesus Christ to come out of her." And *he came out that very hour* (16:16-18, emphasis mine).

> So that even handkerchiefs or aprons were brought from his body to the sick, and the diseases left them and the *evil spirits went out of them* (19:12, emphasis mine).

The tremendous results of these encounters included physical healings and dramatic conversions. Each result is consistent with the ministry of an apostle—to change lives after the pattern of the Apostle Jesus, and thereby establish the credibility and authenticity of the Kingdom.

In the emerging apostolic movement, we can expect the kinds of titanic clashes we see in the book of Acts between the company of the apostles and demonic powers to manifest again. Apostles will be attacked by darkness, and they will respond with apostolic anointing and power. Most likely in the United States and in other Western cultures the wicked spirits that drive the growing New Age movement will be the most threatened and reactive to the ministry of the apostle because they seem to be attempting to dominate the spiritual landscape. In Eastern cultures, other kinds of battles may emerge.

Wherever the apostolic movement penetrates, apostles will have to identify and overcome demonic powers. For example, if a team of apostles are sent to Africa, they will likely wrestle with the territorial spirits of witchcraft, murder and idolatry. Eventually, apostles and their intercessors will confront the wicked spirits behind Islam and Buddhism in territorial warfare for the souls of the inhabitants of those regions that have been captive for hundreds of years. It will require the authority and power of the apostolic company to dislodge many of the territorial spirits that rule over various regions of the world. Such evil spirits will be crushed under the feet of the apostles because they have been given power by Jesus (see Luke 10:19).

6. Apostles Release Supernatural Judgments Against Wickedness

Among the most interesting manifestations of supernatural power in the Bible are the two instances in which divine judgment was released against sin through apostles. The first apostles lived in a day not too different from our own. Sin was evident in every form among both the saved and the lost. When these men of power were confronted with sin that challenged God and had to be supernaturally answered, they responded with displays of power and judgment that are awesome and somewhat unsettling to consider.

In Acts 5, Ananias and his wife, Sapphira, were supernaturally slain by God as the apostle Peter presided over their case. Other believers sold their possessions and turned the entire proceeds over to the apostles, but Ananias and Sapphira turned over only a portion, in the pretense that it was all they had. Peter demonstrated a keen word of knowledge and discovered their sin. He accurately prophesied their deaths, becoming both the channel and interpreter of God's judgment. This sovereign decree of God against sin was necessary to ensure that the integrity of God's people would be preserved through a critical foundational season in the newly forming church.

On another occasion, the apostle Paul pronounced the judgment of God against a wicked sorcerer named Elymas (see Acts 13:8-11). When Paul led the proconsul Sergius Paulus to Christ, the Jewish sorcerer and false prophet also known as Bar-Jesus attempted to turn him away from the faith. So wicked and insidious was this effort that Paul prophetically pronounced judgment against him, and immediately he became blind for a season. Some sin is so heinous that God brings immediate judgment. In at least these two cases, God used an apostle to decree His sovereign judgments on sin.

7. Apostles Manifest Supernatural Power to Raise the Dead

Although the apostles were not exempt from death and sickness, they manifested a measurable degree of miraculous power over them. We have already seen that frequently they had the power to cure the sick in the apostolic ministry. That the apostles also moved in the power to raise the dead is often overlooked.

Not every apostle in the New Testament is on record as having raised the dead. We cannot ignore the fact, however, that both the apostle Paul and the apostle Peter raised people from the dead. Jesus had done this and had instructed the apostles to do the same, saying: "Heal the sick, cleanse the lepers, *raise the dead,* cast out demons. Freely you have received, freely give" (Matt. 10:8, emphasis mine). Clearly Christ saw the ability to raise people from the dead as one of the marks of authentic ministry (see 11:5). In Acts 9:36-42, Dorcas was supernaturally raised from the dead and restored to the people who loved her. Many reports of these kinds of miracles are coming from the mission field, and I personally believe we will be hearing much more of this kind of power.

INCREASING OUR FAITH

We need to keep something in mind as we consider these seven basic areas in which apostles demonstrated power in Scripture. We must remember that the diversity of the apostolic calling prevents us from squeezing apostles into a rigid mold that says, "If you don't manifest a particular power, you are not an apostle." Such a position would be foolish. A person may plant churches, raise up spiritual children and spend his or her life on foreign soil, and yet lack some of the manifestations I've included here. We need to be careful not to imply that such a person is not an apostle. Outside of the examples of apostles provided in scripture, I don't know of any people who have experienced all of these seven manifestations. What constitutes an apostle is more a matter of character and calling than charisma.

Still, we should not presume to water down the clear scriptural pattern of apostolic power. Instead, we should ask the Lord to increase our faith, just as the apostles did (see Luke 17:5). We have seen that apostles operate supernaturally to attract large crowds and release mass conversions. They possess the powers of spiritual impartation. Apostles move in the spirit of revelation, and operate in power over sickness, demons and death. They are supernatural because they are filled with and are following a supernatural God.

Certainly this is a challenge for the many thousands of apostles God is calling forth in this hour. The corporate faith of the people of God needs to be stretched to embrace *all* of the manifestations of God's supernatural power as revealed in the apostle. These powers will not come without cost, but are an irreplaceable part of the apostolic ministry, and must be present in the Church during this present renewal. When they are present, we will be on our way toward raising up powerful and progressive *apostolic churches*.

Notes

1. Cindy Jacobs, *Possessing the Gates of the Enemy* (Grand Rapids: Chosen Books, 1991), p. 86.
2. Roland Allen, *Missionary Methods, St. Paul's or Ours?* (Grand Rapids: Eerdmans, 1962), p. 45.

13

PATTERNS FOR APOSTOLIC CHURCHES

EVERYWHERE YOU TURN THESE DAYS, ANOTHER PROGRAM IS BEING PUSHED AS the key to the church's future. Books are being written, and seminars are being held across the nation to initiate pastors and church leaders into the societies of those who are in the know about the latest methods for growth and success. By the thousands, hungry and often discouraged church leaders pay their fees and listen to the experts describe something new and revolutionary.

This can lead to a syndrome I call *success seminar burnout*. The leader gets excited at a seminar, and changes things at his church to conform to what he has been taught. Then the leader attends another seminar and unlearns some of what he learned at the last seminar, while adding other techniques to his repertoire. Soon another exciting seminar comes along, and the cycle repeats itself. Each time the cycle repeats, the leader may get more confused and discouraged, and the congregation may eventually grow skeptical and resistant to change. After having spent a great deal of time and money that produced little results, the leader may become burned out and is no longer open to *any* new input. The laws of degeneration begin to work and he is left in a worse state than when the cycle began.

WRONG PATTERNS, POOR RESULTS

If the leader becomes confused, it is no wonder. Some seminars teach that dynamic leadership is the key to growth; others say leaders should be low key. Some teach that centralizing and multiplying ministries under one roof such as a mall is the key to attracting people. Others teach that decentralizing through multiple cells is the way to go. Some preach powerful messages to lukewarm Christians to stir them to action while others soften the message and pray to be sensitive to the lost who may be present. Some imply that pastors are unnecessary! The contradictions in the area of church growth and ministry success stories are staggering.

Yet a close examination of some of the churches that appear to be examples of growth often reveals that their successes are superficial. Church-growth experts tell us that on the whole, the American church is really not growing. For every growth success story, many others stories tell of churches losing members to fill those churches. Most growth today is transference growth and, as of yet, a dramatic revival of souls being saved has not occurred. Gloriously, a real move of God's Spirit is taking place in other nations such as Korea, Argentina and Brazil, principally because they are following the Biblical pattern for growth. We would do better to study churches outside of America for keys to real conversion growth.

More than anything, pastors today need to look directly to God for the answers. The faulty patterns we have accepted have produced disappointing results. I hear a cry in the heart of leaders today that says, "We want to see the Church be the church—we want to return to the pattern of Scripture." A desire for reality and truth is beautifully birthed out of this frustration and failure. God can begin to work when leaders come to the end of themselves and look to Him.

THE NEW TESTAMENT MANUAL FOR MINISTRY

If we really want to restore the Church and see it reaching its fullest potential, we must return to New Testament patterns. When we return to the *patterns* of the Early Church, we will recover the *power* of the Early Church.

In the coming apostolic movement, the Church will be the vehicle God uses to accomplish His will. The New Testament reveals that the Church is God's instrument and the apple of His eye. He calls us the royal priesthood (see Rev. 1:6; 5:9,10), the holy nation (see 1 Pet. 2:5-9), the Body of Christ (see 1 Cor. 12:27; Col. 1:18), God's heritage (see 1 Pet. 5:3), the temple of God (see Eph. 2:20-22), the bride of Christ (see Eph. 5:22,23) and His peculiar treasure (see 1 Pet. 2:5-9). Jesus loves the Church, and gave Himself completely for its existence (see Eph. 5:25). Nothing will ever be greater in the heart and purpose of God than His Church.

The Church has been imbued by God with an apostolic purpose and destiny. Edward R. Dayton and David A. Fraser skillfully describe the apostolic nature of the Church:

> Because its center is a self-giving, self-revealing God who sends, the Church is inherently missionary. Having been liberated by the power of the Spirit, the church cannot help but make this same liberation available to all the peoples of the earth. It is "outward bound," centered on the triune God and motivated to share his love and compassion for all peoples in all ages. Unless the missionary nature of the church is understood, the meaning and significance of the church is completely obscured.
>
> Many writers have seen mission at the heart of the life of the church; none, however, more graphically than Emil Brunner: "The Church exists by mission as fire exists by burning."[1]

The energized local church will play an indispensable role in the coming apostolic movement. God is raising up a new generation of churches. A church that is new because it is old, and fresh because it is ancient, is arising today. It is exciting to see what is happening around the world as churches explode under the power of the scriptural pattern. These are not program-driven churches, but pattern-directed churches. They are alive with an apostolic spirit, centered in apostolic activity.

EARMARKS OF AN APOSTOLIC CHURCH

Apostolic people put together under apostolic leadership and an apostolic pattern will emerge as an apostolic church that will change the world just as the Early Church did. By way of introduction, consider what these churches are like:

Apostolic churches are churches whose primary concern is reaching all people with Christ. They have a passion to see entire cultures embrace Jesus in His saving, healing and delivering power. Their focus will eliminate anything not directly related to this objective. They will be true salt and light in society.

Apostolic churches are completely committed to the lordship of Jesus. The clear message of the Early Church was: "Nor is there salvation in any other, for there is no other name under heaven given among men by which we must be saved" (Acts 4:12). They gave everything they had to win the lost and take care of each other. The book of Acts emphasizes the lordship of Jesus no less than 110 times, and it is clearly because these believers were entirely sold out. The message of the lordship of Jesus gives apostolic churches the kind of commitment required to change the world.

Apostolic churches are made up of completely activated members of the Body of Christ. They are not held back by any sense of a clergy-laity split. Their people preach, teach, serve and prophesy according to their spiritual giftings as members of the Body. The pattern in Acts shows that the leaders *and* the people shared the ministry. The whole company of apostolic people will be alive and functioning on earth in the apostolic movement.

Apostolic churches have an intense relationship with the Holy Spirit. The difference in the early Christians' lives was their continual pattern of being filled and refilled with the Holy Spirit (see Acts 2:4; 4:8,31; 7:55; 11:24ff). This was a company of people totally imbued with the power and presence of the Spirit (see 1:8; 2:15). They experienced supernatural power because they were deeply devoted to prayer, fasting, spiritual gifts and faith. It not surprising they were as effective as they were.

NEW TESTAMENT-PATTERN CHURCHES

The one thing the apostles did was to start churches. What effect did these churches have? What can we learn by studying the churches of the first apostolic movement? Let's look briefly at some of these early churches and the patterns they left for us.

Samaria: Influencing the city. Great miracles became a key to founding the church at Samaria under the deacon Philip, whom we have already viewed as an apostolic person (see Acts 8:1-5). Social and racial barriers began to be removed as the Spirit of God flowed into this city, which the Jews viewed as third rate. The legacy of the church at Samaria was its effect on society. Apostolic churches engrave themselves on the tablets of their cities and change the appearance of things forever.

Philippi: The importance of women, joy and giving. The first house church was established from a small group of praying women at Philippi (see 16:6-40). Here another woman who had a spirit of divination was miraculously delivered. When Paul and Silas were imprisoned in the aftermath of her conversion, they sang at midnight and were powerfully set free. The rough jailer who watched over them and his whole family were soon converted. This church later became an example to the other churches of giving support to the apostolic work of Paul (see Phil. 4:15). Apostolic churches are financially committed to apostles and their vision. They sacrifice and give with joy, and experience the blessing of God that comes with that sacrifice.

Thessalonica: Thriving amid resistance. Thessalonica became a church built amid extreme opposition. From its inception, Paul's persuasive ministry in Thessalonica was opposed (see Acts 17:1-7; 1 Thess. 2:2). Hindrances did not stop the church from becoming a great center of ministry, noted by the apostle as a model church (see 1 Thess. 1:7,8). True apostolic churches do not buckle under pressure, whether that pressure is political, financial or spiritual. Instead, they thrive, as at Thessalonica, even under the worst of conditions.

Berea: Building on the Word. Though we do not know much else about it, the church established at Berea encourages all of us to eagerly receive the taught Word, while carefully examining it (see Acts 17:11). The Christians there were described as noble, and inspire every church in terms of their response to the Word of God. Every church that God establishes in the apostolic movement will be grounded and balanced in the Word of God. Apostolic churches are not characterized by trends as much as truth. They are full of the "present truth" revelation of God (2 Pet. 1:12).

Corinth: Establishing order and holiness. The church at Corinth, though somewhat famous for its many excesses, became a place for the apostle Paul to prove and develop many essential teachings and experiences. Our greatest insights into the life of stewardship, holiness, spiritual power and ability, church structure and authority find their roots in the fertile soil at Corinth. Like the church at Corinth, apostolic churches will not be perfect, but they will be properly ordered and growing in the holiness of God.

Ephesus: Structured for growth, order and longevity. Ephesus became an important center of ministry for both Paul and John. The church there grew to gigantic proportions, and lasted many decades as a hub of apostolic activity. Several structural and outreach strategies were modeled for us at Ephesus: the plurality of eldership was well established in this church (see Acts 20:29,30); home meetings were part of the congregation's life (see v. 20); financial support of apostolic ministry (see Eph. 20:29-34) was also key. Ephesus patterns several important things, not the least of which is excellence in structure. Apostolic churches will be well structured for growth, order and longevity.

Colosse: Triumphing over heresy. The church at Colosse is a monument to surviving pervasive heresy. The problems at Colosse of philosophy (see Col. 2:8), legalism (see vv. 14-16), mysticism (see v. 18) and asceticism (see vv. 20-22) nearly choked the life out of the church, but through proper teaching and apostolic correction, it went on to thrive for an extended period of fruitful ministry. The pervasive influences of the New Age highlights the importance for modern apostolic churches to prepare to triumph over heresy and deception as centers of life-giving truth.

Rome: Establishing new centers of outreach. Much can be said about the church at Rome and its legacy to us. Space would not allow for a complete discussion of the church at Rome, but it can be said here that Rome was a base of operation for the faith for many generations. The apostle Paul longed to visit and have this strategic center of outreach established (see Rom. 1:8-11). It became the gateway to the Western world for the gospel, and remains a testament to the powerful role one city can play in God's plan for spreading the gospel to the nations. New Testament apostolic churches will resemble the church at Rome because they will reach beyond themselves. An apostolic church reaches out and bears fruit.

Although each of these churches contributed significantly to the life of the Church, two important churches in the New Testament influenced the world for God in apostolic ministry: Jerusalem and Antioch.

JERUSALEM: THE PROTOTYPICAL APOSTOLIC CHURCH

The Church had its beginnings in Jerusalem. The Church was birthed there at Pentecost in approximately A.D. 33. From virtually nothing, the Church of Jesus Christ experienced a glorious identity. Thousands were saved and added to the Church in the days that followed Pentecost. This necessitated that the early practices of organizing the church take place in fairly rapid sequence. The apostles gathered in Jerusalem and made many decisions there (see Acts 15). In every sense of the word, the Church was pioneered and established in the Holy City, which became the mother church for all the initial churches, and as such the church at Jerusalem became a pattern for all other churches to follow.

Some of the most dynamic patterns for the Church emerged from Jerusalem. We see apostles operating in Jerusalem. We see an apostolic people forming who are vibrant and alive with the power of God. The Church developed a certain structural and organizational order in Jerusalem.

The patterns of Acts 2:42 were the most significant. In Jerusalem "they continued steadfastly in the apostles' doctrine and fellowship, in the breaking of bread, and in prayers." Without these essential elements in place, the church at Jerusalem, and indeed any church, could not have survived and flourished. The *apostles' doctrine* was Jesus Christ, the risen Lord (see Acts 5:28,42; 9:20; 15:35; 2 John 9). The *fellowship* that flowed in the Early Church was an intimacy with God through the Spirit, not just a religious commitment (see 1 Cor. 1:9; 2 Cor. 13:14; Phil. 3:10). The *breaking of bread* was a common meal around the Lord's Table that signified the transforming redemption and forgiveness of Christ flowing within the life of the Church (see Matt. 26:29; Mark 14:25; Acts 10:41). The element of *prayer* was the recognized source of all power within the Jerusalem church (see Acts 3:1; 6:4). These essential foundations were laid at the Jerusalem church as a pattern for every church.

ANTIOCH: THE PROGRESSIVE APOSTOLIC CHURCH

The Church is far more than an organization. It is an organism—living, changing and growing. Rather than being frozen in time, it develops and adapts to changing circumstances while retaining its essential nature and mission. The church at Jerusalem cannot be understood as the final pattern for all churches to follow. Other churches followed Jerusalem and made important gains in many ways.

Although the church at Jerusalem was the prototypical apostolic church, it only existed for a little more than three decades. The Romans destroyed the city of Jerusalem in A.D. 70, and the remaining Christians were completely scattered. Jerusalem as a church was no longer a central gathering place. The church had to spread out and find new centers of ministry. Nothing remained of the church except the pattern that was in people's minds.

At some point after Pentecost, an unnamed group of disciples came to Antioch from Jerusalem. They formed a church consisting of new converts from Judaism and society at large, until many believers came together. When the apostles and elders from Jerusalem heard of this phenomenal growth, they sent Barnabas to assist. Soon, Barnabas enlisted Saul of Tarsus (not yet accepted in Jerusalem) to help with the work at Antioch.

Soon Antioch became the hub of activity in the lives of the apostles. It became the base of operations for the apostles Paul and Barnabas; in Antioch the Holy Spirit ordained and sent them forth. In each of Paul's three apostolic journeys, Antioch was the point of departure and the place of return. The church at Antioch covered his ministry with prayer and financial help, and it no doubt became Paul's spiritual home. As such, the church at Antioch was the fountainhead from which most of the churches of the New Testament sprang, and the first church organized to send out apostles and other ministries to evangelize the world.

Referring to the tremendous importance of the church at Antioch, Dr. McBirnie asserts, "The greatest missionary and the greatest evangelist who ever lived was St. Paul. Antioch was his home base. This is where the Holy Spirit said, 'Now separate Paul and Barnabas unto Me and send them.' The church people obediently dug into their pockets, came up with the money, and sent them. Paul started churches like a string of pearls all over the route of the circle which he traveled on his first journey, but the pearls led back home and clasped together at Antioch."[2]

The beautiful patterns in Jerusalem were expanded and improved at Antioch over a period of time. The prototype was enhanced and transformed into a progressive pattern for future churches to follow.

Antioch differed from Jerusalem, which became a missionary church, largely as a result of persecution. Antioch was a missionary church in the twofold sense that it was founded by missionaries and in turn became a missionary base for sending the gospel to regions beyond. As far as is known, it was the first church to engage in fulfilling the last portion of Christ's commission to be witnesses to the ends of the earth.[3]

PATTERNS PRACTICED AT ANTIOCH

Several outstanding things about Antioch could be cited as reasons for its tremendous influence on the world. Jerusalem was to remain important in the worldwide Christian community until the Roman army destroyed the city in A.D. 70, and Paul reported back to the believers there after each of his missionary journeys abroad. The church at Antioch, however, actually set the pattern for the future.[4] Antioch was a remarkable center of apostolic activity, and offered many usable patterns for today.[5]

Commitment (Acts 11:29)

The believers at Antioch were known as disciples, meaning they were disciplined learners and followers of Jesus Christ. They acknowledged Jesus as Lord and denied themselves, taking up their crosses daily (see Luke 9:23). Many of them left the comforts of their own surroundings to travel and evangelize for the Lord.

Grace (v. 23)

When Barnabas was sent to observe the believers' faith, he encountered a strong grace upon all of them. This church was not infected with the legalism that threatened the other churches of the first century. They knew the grace of the Lord Jesus Christ, and functioned in His life-changing power continually.

Benevolence (vv. 29,30)

When Jerusalem was hit by famine, the believers in Antioch responded by sending relief. Because of their determination to help the brethren who were suffering in Jerusalem, immediately a mass collection was received and given to the apostles to distribute. This act of benevolence is a testimony to the believers' purity of faith and love for God (see James 1:27).

Spirituality (13:1,2)
The Holy Spirit was freely moving and speaking in the church at Antioch. The saints there sought God for the direction of the ministry, and the Holy Spirit supernaturally spoke in clear terms. Great power was imparted through the Holy Spirit as men laid their hands on the apostles and sent them out to the ripened harvest field.

Diversity (v. 1)
Barnabas was a Jew and a Levite. Simeon (called Niger, literally "black") was likely a black man. Lucius, probably a Gentile, was from the African colony of Cyrene. Manaen was from the privileged levels of society, having a close childhood connection with Herod the Tetrarch. Saul was a former Jewish Pharisee who was highly educated, and who grew up in a strongly Gentile environment. Yet all of these men, who were racially and socially different from one another, were counted among the same company of prophets and teachers. There was no segregation or bigotry at Antioch. By all appearances, these varied lives blended beautifully into a ministry team that changed the course of world history.

Giftedness (v. 1)
Certain men in residence at Antioch oversaw significant and recognized ministries. Included were prophets, elders, teachers and disciples. Apostles and evangelists such as Paul and Barnabas were sent out from Antioch. We can safely assume that such a church would have several pastors there as well. Many people were assembled there, each possessing the gifts of the Holy Spirit.

Teaching (11:26; 13:1)
By "teaching" we mean that doctrinal instruction was a priority in Antioch. For example, Paul and Barnabas taught the church for a period of one whole year, strengthening the believers in the Word of God. Among the pronounced ministries, other teachers were present and active in the church.

Prophetic Ministry (13:1)
Clearly this church at Antioch was a church staffed and led by the

prophets. The church at Antioch listened to the prophets who forecasted famine (see 11:27-30), and they listened to the prophets in selecting Paul and Barnabas. Considering all the potential missionaries and missionary activity that could have been initiated, the leaders at Antioch waited for the prophetic directive before they invested their men and money. Once the prophets spoke, however, the church moved accordingly.

Worship (v. 2)
When the Christians at Antioch gathered, their first activity was to minister to the Lord. The people depicted in Acts 13 appear determined to worship God, allowing the prophetic and evangelistic vision to be birthed in that experience. After all, if we fail in prioritizing worship, we cannot hope to possess prophetic power or evangelistic effect.

Prayer (v. 2)
The people prayed and fasted until they heard from God. Their missionary activity was born in a prayer meeting. Their worship took place in a prayer meeting. The Holy Spirit spoke clearly to them in a prayer meeting. Jesus said the Church He was building would be a house of prayer (see Matt. 21:13), and Antioch seems to have been no exception.

Structure (vv. 2,3)
We see the presidency of the Holy Spirit initiating, directing and speaking to a people who followed and understood spiritual authority. Leaders were flowing in major decision-making processes, and no one moved in a disorderly or disrespectful way. Every leader maintained a proper relationship to authority, and the Holy Spirit led them beautifully into unanimous action.

Impartation (v. 3)
Before Paul and Barnabas were sent forth from Antioch, fasting, prayer and the laying on of hands were employed to impart strength to them. The believers there understood the significance of the laying on of hands, and had something spiritually real to give to the apostles they sent out. Later, Paul would lay his hands on other world changers such as Timothy (see 2 Tim. 1:6), imparting the gift of God he had received from those whose hands were laid on him.

Apostolic Passion (v. 3)

From this single congregation of Christians the most dynamic churches of the ancient world were planted. The life and power of Antioch was not confined to Antioch, but was constantly exported through wave after wave of apostolic teams who would affect their world. Teams were sent, regions were evangelized and churches were established, all because of the vision Antioch possessed for other cities and places.

SUMMARY

As we study the church at Antioch, we see an important pattern of growth and ministry emerge. This pattern challenges us to minister on an entirely different level from traditional ministries. Antioch was effective because it understood these key principles of ministry and practiced them, releasing ministry around the known world. Jerusalem waited until persecution hit before it scattered itself. Antioch, however, heard the Spirit and followed the pattern of duplicating itself wherever its ministries went.

Each church of the New Testament reveals a unique aspect of the full pattern God has for the Church today. Rather than imitating superficial success and committing to unscriptural methods, leaders today need to return to the New Testament plan. We must "make all things according to the pattern" (Heb. 8:5). Planting and watering spiritually invigorated local churches is a key to the coming apostolic movement, and the pattern prepares us to become a living part of *the Kingdom net*.

Notes
1. Edward R. Dayton and David A. Fraser, *Planning Strategies for World Evangelization* (Grand Rapids: Eerdmans, 1980), p. 59.
2. William Steuart McBirnie, *The Search for the Early Church* (Wheaton, Ill.: Tyndale House, 1978), p. 48.
3. Everet F. Harrison, *The Apostolic Church* (Grand Rapids: Eerdmans, 1985), p. 188.
4. Tim Dowley, John H. Y. Briggs, Robert D. Linder and David F. Wright, eds., *Eerdmans Handbook to the History of Christianity* (Grand Rapids: 1977), p. 62.
5. This outline is adapted from a teaching codeveloped by the author and Dr. Emanuele Cannistraci in the church pamphlet entitled "Catch the Vision of the House: The Antioch Principle," available from Evangel Christian Fellowship, 1255 Pedro Street, San Jose, California 95126.

14

THE KINGDOM NET

A WORLDWIDE TREND IS EMERGING IN OUR DAY THAT IS RADICALLY CHANGing the way business, politics and information services operate. Explosive advances are being made because people are connecting to increase benefits for everyone. The trend is called "networking," and many agree that it is the wave of the future because it is so effective.

WHAT IS NETWORKING?

Networking is something of a miracle. On March 13, 1995, two American civilians, William Barloon and David Daliberti, who worked in Kuwait, accidentally strayed across the border into Iraq in an attempt to visit some friends. When they realized they had violated Iraq's boundaries, they tried to reenter Kuwait, but were immediately arrested as criminals and sentenced to eight years in jail. Their families back home were shocked and torn in anguish at the prospect of this horrible mishap.

In the midst of their pain, a computer was donated to one of the wives. It was connected to the internet, a worldwide web of information systems, and within moments, previously impossible support was available to her. From her living room, she was able to communicate hourly with the American embassy in Iraq. She could check with the military to verify the status of her husband. When any news developed, she could be immediately notified. When a computer address was assigned to her, computer users throughout the world began to transmit sympathy, comfort and prayers to her screen. Thankfully, on July 16, 1995, the two men were released.

This story illustrates a striking fact: Through the power of networking, this grieving woman was able to ask the world for help as easily as she could ask her neighbor. And through networking, the world answered back at minimal cost, and in real time. Networking had performed its miracle.

In the broad sense, networking is simply enhancing life by sharing resources through relationships and connections. Networking depends on these relationships and connections as the core of its power. The miracle of networking is the unlimited potential it has for bringing previously isolated things together for beneficial exchanges and marvelous accomplishments. Networking is becoming so valuable that soon financial worth may not be measured in terms of money, but in terms of the network of connections.[1]

NETWORKS ARE HERE!

The productive use of networking principles in our world is nothing short of revolutionary. Network organizations are replacing organizations built around traditional hierarchies.[2] The growing trend of network marketing makes products available through relationships between families, friends and business associates instead of depending on high-overhead practices such as advertising or displays. Television and radio networks have long combined resources to broadcast programming, share the load of covering local events and sell advertising time within affiliated stations. Phone systems interconnect billions of miles of wire and satellite signals through worldwide networks, enabling millions of callers to access phones and transmit data simultaneously from anywhere on the planet. Computer networks integrate various data systems that instantly access voluminous information otherwise unavailable.

This process has become so productive that one of Washington's great ambitions involves completing the "information superhighway," which will forever change the way our nation operates. The scenario of the woman whose husband was arrested in Iraq could be repeated in millions of different versions throughout the world every day. The world truly is getting smaller. Networking is powerful, and it is here to stay.

THE GREATEST NETWORK

Like so many successes in our day, networking succeeds because God invented it. Networking is a reflection of the divine pattern of interdependence and unity God has ordained for the Church. The Body of Christ is, in essence, the greatest network ever invented. As a powerful network of human lives, it depends on the strength of its relational connections to fulfill the Great Commission.

The images in Scripture of the Church as a Body reflect the Body of Christ as a network:

> From whom the whole body, joined and knit together by what every joint supplies, according to the effective working by which every part does its share, causes growth of the body for the edifying of itself in love (Eph. 4:16).

> Now I plead with you, brethren, by the name of our Lord Jesus Christ, that you all speak the same thing, and that there be no divisions among you, but that you be perfectly joined together in the same mind and in the same judgment (1 Cor. 1:10).

The New Testament abounds with practical applications of networking. The Early Church networked to share resources so effectively that not one among many thousands lacked for anything (see Acts 4:34,35). The pattern continued as the apostles came together to network at the Jerusalem Council in Acts 15. Since the earliest days of the Church, the Kingdom has grown upon a foundation of combined effort and relational unity.

This paradigm needs to be recovered today. If the pattern of networking is recaptured and reproduced in the Church today, I am convinced that our effectiveness can equal—and even surpass—that of the Early Church.

THE KINGDOM NET

The words of Jesus validate the Kingdom net. In a powerful illustration, Jesus declared a dynamic reality: "The kingdom of heaven is like unto a net" (Matt. 13:47, *KJV*).

When Jesus spoke to the people who were gathered on the shores of Galilee, He skillfully painted a picture in their minds of the huge dragnets that were commonly used in that day. Thousands of connecting knots held the net together and made it an amazing tool. The net was placed in the waters, and its ends were stretched out and drawn together to gather huge quantities of fish. That same picture needs to surface in our minds. We need to view the kingdom of God as a giant net.

How is the Kingdom of heaven like a net? The net illustrates how increase becomes possible when God's people are joined together like the interconnecting cords of a net. As the Body of Christ links in interconnecting relationships and shares resources, we become powerful tools for catching lost souls. Without these quality connections, our effectiveness is diminished. Like any good net, our ability to cause increase depends on our connection with one another. This is the substance of the net of the Kingdom.

APOSTLES AND NETWORKING

As the apostolic movement gains momentum, the practice of networking has begun to flourish again in the Body of Christ. Church-growth analysts are beginning to identify *apostolic networks* as a modern movement. World-changing leaders and movements are arising to establish progressive structures for families of churches and ministries. The weaknesses of traditional denominationalism are succumbing to the strengths of apostolic networks.

Leaders and churches have long sought this kind of unity and cooperation. The existence of many denominations attests to this fact. Unfortunately, history's harsh lesson has revealed that the structures upholding most denominations often undermine the purpose of unity, thus creating division and breakdown. Many believe that two effects are evidenced by this problem—denominationalism is slowly dying, and an antidenominational feeling is arising. Many people now mistakenly equate "organized religion" with evil, and resist any structure at all. Both developments are unfortunate.

Today, it appears that the people of God are moving toward a marvelous balance between spiritual structures without organization and those with too much organization. We are acknowledging our need to connect in a way that produces life. The apostolic network is becoming the answer to that cry.

APOSTOLIC TEAM MINISTRY

What prototype of apostolic networking do we find in Scripture? How does the process of the growth of the Body of Christ work in tangible terms? Simply put, the biblical template of *apostolic team ministry* is an embryonic application of the apostolic network idea. Since the time that the apostles were sent by Jesus in pairs (see Mark 6:7), apostolic ministry has involved teamwork. Jesus chose a team of 12 men with whom to share His work. And the usual pattern for ministry in the book of Acts is always team ministry.

Apostles never worked alone. Paul and Barnabas formed a team with their companions (see Acts 13:4—15:12). Later the team of Judas and Silas joined the team of Paul and Barnabas, forming a larger team (see 15:22-34). After Paul and Barnabas parted, two teams emerged, including the team of Barnabas and Mark (see vv. 37-39) and the team of Paul and Silas (see v. 40), who were later joined by Timothy, Luke, Aquila, Priscilla and Apollos (see 16:3-9,10; 18:2-30). Other apostolic team players included Erastus, Gaius and Aristarchus in Acts 19, and Sopater, Secundus, Tychicus and Trophimus in Acts 20. It is abundantly clear that the New Testament pattern for apostolic ministry is a pattern of teamwork.

This simple fact becomes the conceptual foundation for modern apostolic networks.[3] A network is an extension of the team-ministry principle which brought together the variety of apostles, pastors, prophets, teachers and evangelists that were necessary to plant and establish churches throughout the known world.

That apostles teamed up for ministry reveals something important to us about their philosophy of ministry. True apostles are people who are willing to merge their gifts with the gifts of others in the Body of Christ to properly establish the Kingdom. Apostles and prophets have a unique blending of gifts and often work together in this regard (see Luke 11:49; Eph. 2:20; 3:5; Rev. 18:20). While working together can pose difficulties, as it did with Paul and Barnabas (see Acts 15:2), apostles are essentially relational men who understand that they need the rest of the Body of Christ.

WHAT IS AN APOSTOLIC NETWORK?

An apostolic network can take many forms. Essentially, it is a band of autonomous churches and individual ministries that are voluntarily united in an organized structure. This framework of human relationships is sufficient to facilitate interdependency between network members and their apostolic oversight. Network members possess a common vision and demonstrate a tangible expression of New Testament apostolic ministry. Although each network may accomplish organization through varied methods, values, philosophies and goals, they all share the essence of connecting relationships and combining resources. "The network becomes a melting pot of strategy, vision, methods, teaching, training and programs."[4]

Apostolic networks are different from most denominations because in networks, *relationships* (not policies and rules) are the main source of organizational strength. Only minimal legal and financial control are imposed. In the apostolic network to which I belong, the function of government is accomplished largely through the partnership of prayer, discussion, planning and visionary leadership. The most effective networks are more than mere ministerial fellowships, because the purpose is to accomplish apostolic ministry and not to merely facilitate camaraderie.

BASIC ELEMENTS
OF AN APOSTOLIC NETWORK

What makes an apostolic network a network? Several essential elements can be identified.

A Recognized Apostle or Team of Apostles in Leadership

Every network organization needs an overseer who acts as the catalyst and ultimate strategist of the network. Ideally, the overseer works with an apostolic team structure in the network's government, networking with prophets and other gift ministries according to scriptural patterns. Together, they form a team of servant-leaders who act as facilitators for the network's vision and purpose. This cannot be a traditional autocratic hierarchy, but must be structured upon a philosophy of servant-hood that permeates leadership at every level in the network. The oversight of an apostle holds the entire network together relationally. Roland Allen says of the Early Church, "It was held together, not merely by convenience, not merely by common faith and common sacraments, but also by common submission to a common founder. The unity of the churches in the different provinces was expressed not only in constant intercourse one with another, but by their common recognition of the Apostle's authority as the messenger of Christ to them."[5] The first ingredient builds a foundation for the other three.

An Atmosphere of Dynamic Relationships

John Dawson, a best-selling author, rightly says, "God organizes His kingdom through gifts of friendship."[6] Relationships are the most essential key to networking. Anything built on rules and control is destined to fail. Some denominations have become progressively oppressive because rules and policies are relied upon to maintain the integrity of the structure instead of carefully maintaining relationships. Love and voluntary cooperation is the essence and spirit of the network. It is the difference between an organization and a living organism. The relationships must not be symbolic or mystical; they must be tangible and real to maintain the net's integrity. Frequent time together in conferences, events and gatherings can perpetuate this essential element of a network.

Apostolic leader John Kelly teaches that preserving a balanced and up-to-date network requires that the apostle maintain fellowship with apostles outside of his own stream. No true network can succeed as a closed system.[7]

A Distinct Mission and Purpose

Without a vision, people perish (see Prov. 29:18). Purpose is essential to the survival of a network. A clear and compelling mission is the guiding light of an apostolic network.

Frank Damazio pinpoints the priority of mission within true spiritual movements. "When people willingly come together to accomplish a mission they create a movement. The movement grows when its members are trained and mobilized to propagate the mission. It is up to the leadership to continually identify and articulate the mission."[8] To avoid becoming lost in the doldrums, this mission needs to transcend mere fellowship, and instead center on church planting, outreach and world missions. A written document is a helpful way to communicate the mission to network members. Mission is the heart of a properly structured network.

A Gathering of Apostolic Churches

Local churches are the organizational backbone of the network model because they are at the heart of the apostolic ministry itself. Like all organizations, networks justify their existence by producing a tangible end product. The local church is that product. Because the primary work of an apostle is to plant and water churches, an apostolic network will of necessity be composed of properly structured and committed apostolic churches made up of apostolic people willing to pray, give and go. Network churches are not under the rule of the network, but are autonomous and self-supporting. They should be held together by a mutual compatibility of mission, values and doctrine.

Loving apostolic headship and kingdom-focused objectives are foundational to successful apostolic networks. Three balanced priorities create the wholeness of the apostolic network.

THREE ESSENTIAL PRIORITIES FOR APOSTOLIC NETWORKING

An extensive look at the Kingdom net analogy will assist us in understanding the primary components of apostolic networks: relationship, training and mission.

1. Relationship

Apostolic networks must maintain the relational priority. As we have seen, the Body of Christ is really a living network. If any member becomes relationally dislocated, the network cannot be sound. The Kingdom cannot act as a true net unless believers take their places and become what God has created them to be in one another's lives.

People coming together in relationship create the kingdom net, and walking in the truth of God's Word *washes the net*. Natural nets get dirty. Slimy weeds and sediments will clog and tangle the net. A net must be cleansed to remain useful.

How does the Kingdom net get cleansed? The apostle John gave the answer; it is the power of relationship! "But if we walk in the light as He is in the light, we have fellowship with one another, and the blood of Jesus Christ His Son cleanses us from all sin" (1 John 1:7). Something happens when God's people get together in radiant fellowship. Fellowship refines us and produces the glow of purity in our lives. When we fail to fellowship, we can become polluted with wrong thoughts, sins and misconceptions. An apostolic network that lacks the horizontal element of life in the Spirit will lack the strength and purity needed to accomplish great things.

2. Equipping and Reproduction

Another strength in networking lies in constantly reproducing ministry so the net can expand. A lot of work needs to be done and we need an ever-expanding net to draw in the catch.

The New Testament pattern of equipping people for ministry is what *mends the net*: "And He Himself gave some to be apostles, some prophets, some evangelists, and some pastors and teachers, for the equipping of the saints for the work of ministry, for the edifying of the body of Christ" (Eph. 4:11,12).

Nets can become torn and tattered from use. Our relationships, gifts and abilities need to be constantly mended and improved for greater effectiveness.

The root word for "perfecting" is *katartizo*, meaning "to render fit, complete."[9] In Mark 1:19 it is translated "mend," speaking of torn, damaged nets. In Galatians 6:1, it is translated "restore," speaking of those who are overtaken in a fault. It speaks of taking care of that which is useful for drawing others in. If the net is to be useful it must be maintained. That is the job of the ministry—to maintain and equip the Body for usefulness. The successful network is mended constantly through leaders who guide and strengthen God's people. An apostolic network that lacks the element of training and equipping will not outlive its current constituency. It will die with its members and fail to accomplish its purpose.

3. Mission

Expansion and growth are the immutable mandates of the Kingdom. When we go forth into all the world, we are essentially *casting the*

Kingdom net. For a net to be effective, it must be placed in the water! For the Body of Christ to be effective, we must be immersed in the world. As God's net, our mission is to catch fish by casting ourselves into the sea of lost humanity in total abandon.

Preaching the gospel of the Kingdom is *pulling in the net.* Once the net is in the water, it has to be reeled in to collect the fish.[10] Unless our Kingdom net draws people into the Kingdom and into the house of the Lord, no catching and changing of lives can occur. The local church is responsible for receiving the fish that are caught as a visible expression of God's kingdom.

These priorities need to be practiced if the Kingdom-net principle is to find a use in the ministry of the apostle and in the emerging apostolic movement. Once this is in place, new opportunities for increase will present themselves.

THE NEXT STEP: NETWORKING NETWORKS

An even higher level of networking is on the horizon for the Church. Networks forming in the emerging apostolic movement will noticeably benefit the Body of Christ. Consider how these same benefits could increase in quantum force if the various networks could connect *with each other* in relationships and shared resources. What could be accomplished by *networking networks*?

What is the biblical outline for this kind of connection? It is nothing less than the unity of all believers! (see Eph. 4:3,5; John 17:21; 1 Cor. 1:10).

The marvelous prospect of worldwide biblical unity could begin with apostles and heads of networks coming together for prayer, strategy and relationship. Efforts could be coordinated and ideas shared in dynamic and expansive dimensions. Perhaps this wisdom inspired the heads of the tribes in Israel to gather long ago (see Deut. 33:5).

One example of an attempt to unite apostles occurred in the United States. It was the popular charismatic Network of Christian Ministries (NCM). While the apostolic movement is not limited to the charismatic wing of the Church, I use this example because it was a noble attempt to unify at least a major portion of the Church. The NCM had its origin in 1982 when network founders Emanuele Cannistraci (my uncle and spiritual father), Mel Davis, John Gimenez and Charles Green discussed the need for a network that would blend the major streams of the charismatic movement in relational unity and harmony.

The network was organized into a governing body of leaders. The leaders brought together every part of the classical Pentecostal, neo-Pentecostal and charismatic church streams. I was present at the network's initial gathering in Denver, Colorado, in July 1985. The gathering was electrified by the presence of God. A heavy prophetic anointing was present. Love and unity filled the atmosphere. Many of the leaders of the various movements publicly repented for their spirits of suspicion and division toward other major leaders. Prominent men and women of God pled for forgiveness and restoration of fellowship. An unprecedented cleansing and healing occurred in those meetings. Many agreed that the network's potential impact on the corporate Body of Christ was phenomenal.

By the fourth annual conference in 1989 in Anaheim, California, most of the national leaders of the charismatic renewal were involved. Sadly, the network did not survive. In my conversations with him about this network, Dr. Cannistraci identified the network's breakup as a result not of disunity, lack of enthusiasm or love for one another, but of a failure to answer the cry of the "spiritual sons" for fathering. During one fragile moment in that conference, several spiritual sons lifted up a collective appeal for the spiritual fathers to assume their roles as mentors to the younger generation of world changers. The sons were calling for a movement of the fathers. It was an awesome occasion, according to Dr. Cannistraci. Tragically, the cry was never fully answered.

"The missing ingredient was fathers coming together with their giftings and reservoirs of knowledge, networking to pass on the legacy to the younger generation. Networking can be far more powerful if the fathers are available to the sons" says Dr. Cannistraci. "Without that ingredient, a network will be short-lived." We need to search for networks manifesting this ingredient and then seek to model ourselves after those networks.

Gloriously, new networks are emerging in this hour throughout the world. Particularly in third world countries, we are seeing an explosion of not only apostolic ministry, but apostolic organizations and networks. With God's help, a new generation of networks will arise to carry the torch that was lit in part through the Network of Christian Ministries.

Once Kingdom-networks begin to network, the possible advantages for the Church become enormous. I believe when the Body of Christ reaches this level, *entire nations can be taken,* as they were in the early decades of the Church. This is apostolic ministry at its zenith. We could develop a spirit of harmony in doctrine and morals, such as was achieved in Jerusalem among the apostles. The power of multiple networks voluntarily moving in the same direction paves the way for efforts in famine relief, ministry mobilization and sharing resources in greater dimensions than ever before.

Imagine what would happen if the leading apostles came together, heard from God and committed the resources of their networks to reach a particular nation or people group! This kind of power could sweep the planet and reap the worldwide harvest almost overnight. As the apostolic stream of restoration flows ever stronger, we must keep this potential in mind. It may well be one of the tools God uses to consummate His plan for our planet.

APOSTLES AND CORPORATE UNITY

Today we are all concerned about the important issue of church unity. As a result, an increasing number of noble efforts have been made to foster understanding, forgiveness and reconciliation in the Body of Christ. In some ways, we are beginning to see the desired unity take root, but the Body of Christ is still largely fragmented.

Restoration of the ministry of apostles is intrinsic to church unity. Apostles, along with the other ministry gifts, were given by Christ to edify the Church and to bring it to the *unity of the faith* (see Eph. 4:11-13). If the office of the apostle is not restored, how can we hope for unity? The apostle is part of the fivefold cord God has created to tie the Body of Christ together in unity. George R. Hatwin, a Canadian teacher active in the 1940s and '50s, wrote, "There shall never be any unity of faith until the ministry of the true apostle is recognized and obeyed as strictly in the last days as it was obeyed in the days of the apostle Paul."[11]

He went on to note, "Any attempts to pray, organize, reconcile, or repent will be inadequate to produce church unity unless the apostles emerge, for apostolic ministry is the very essence of unity."[12] In this context, then, apostolic networking is an indispensable part of God's end-time purpose in the Church.

SUMMARY

Networking has swept the world with its effectiveness. It is important that we experience a similar revolution in the Church. Certainly the future task is great; consequently, we cannot afford to overlook something as central to our success as practical unity. Doubtless, without applying the principles of networking, apostolic ministry will not be sufficient to achieve world evangelization. No one can do it alone, but together we can accomplish anything.

The Church presently possesses a wealth of vision, spiritual gifts and talents, human resources, money and ideas, but we are not managing them effectively. If we return to the miracle of the Body of Christ through relational and organizational networking, the outcome will be awesome. The results could be as miraculous as the Kingdom net itself.

Notes

1. Wayne E. Baker, *Networking Smart—How to Build Relationships for Personal and Organizational Success* (New York: McGraw-Hill, 1994), p. xv.
2. Ibid., p. xvi.
3. The author gratefully acknowledges the insights gleaned from apostle John Kelly in the area of apostolic networking. John's two informal lectures to the newly forming Antioch Network of Churches and Ministries—July 1992 and April 1993—at which the author was privileged to be present, have provided much of the insight for this section.
4. *Ministries Manual* (Summerville, S.C.: Resurrection Churches and Ministries, 1992), p. B2.
5. Roland Allen, *Missionary Methods, St. Paul's or Ours?* (Grand Rapids: Eerdmans, 1962), p. 127.
6. John Dawson, *Taking Our Cities for God* (Lake Mary, Fla.: Creation House, 1989), p. 108.
7. *Ministries Manual*, p. C1.
8. Frank Damazio, *The Vanguard Leader* (Portland, Oreg.: Bible Temple, 1994), p. 54.
9. Larry Lea with Judy Doyle, *Mending Broken Nets and Broken Fishermen* (Rockwall, Tex.: Church On The Rock, 1985), p. 13.
10. Ibid., p. 92.
11. George R. Hatwin, "The Ministry of an Apostle," *The Sharon Star* (April/May 1951): 1.
12. Ibid.

CONCLUSION

If we are right in anticipating an unprecedented revival in our generation, we may be standing on history's holiest ground. No other generation has had the privilege of living in an hour like ours. Right before our eyes, we are witnessing a world-changing wave forming on the horizon, heading straight for our shores. An outpouring is upon us. We can feel the latter rain falling, and see the tender leaf springing up. *The harvest is near.*

We are living in the early stages of a great apostolic movement, and are experiencing a rebirth of the ministry of the apostle. Jesus is calling thousands of sent ones to arise in this hour. A great apostolic company is arising.

Now is the time to return to the patterns and experiences found in His Word. We must recover all that has been lost so the harvest can be brought in, and the wave can take us to new places as the triumphant Church.

Today, the Spirit of God calls us to action:

> *Apostolic people, go change the world.*
> *Churches, receive a renewing from the Apostolic Spirit.*
> *Pastors, see that you build according to the pattern.*
> *Fathers, take your places in the family of God.*

Our fervent prayer now becomes:

> *Let the earth witness the supernatural power of God.*

Let the nations be planted and watered.
Let the enemy be displaced.
Let the kingdom net be drawn in.

The Lord of the Harvest quickly answers:

"Let the apostles come forth!"

BIBLIOGRAPHY

Allen, Roland. *Missionary Methods, St. Paul's or Ours?* Grand Rapids: Eerdmans, 1962.

Baker, Wayne E. *Networking Smart—How to Build Relationships for Personal and Organizational Success.* New York: McGraw-Hill, 1994.

Benjamin, Dick, "Here's What the Bible Says About Women's Ministries." *The Gospel Truth* (July/August 1980).

Bilezikian, Gilbert. *Beyond Sex Roles.* Grand Rapids: Baker, 1985.

Bruce, F. F. *Paul: Apostle of the Heart Set Free.* Grand Rapids: Eerdmans, 1977.

Burgess, Stanley M., and Gary B. McGee, eds. *The Dictionary of Pentecostal and Charismatic Movements.* Grand Rapids: Zondervan, 1988.

Chadwick, Henry. *The Early Church.* England: Penguin Books, 1967.

Christian Equippers International. *The Master Builder* (1985).

Conner, Kevin J. The Church in the New Testament. Australia: Acacia Press, 1982.

Cross, F. L., ed. The Oxford Dictionary of the Christian Church. Oxford: The Oxford University Press, 1983.

Damazio, Frank. The Making of a Leader. Portland, Oreg.: Bible Temple, 1980.

———. *The Vanguard Leader.* Portland, Oreg.: Bible Temple, 1994.

Dawson, John. *Taking Our Cities for God.* Lake Mary, Fla.: Creation House, 1989.

Dayton, Edward R., and David A. Fraser. *Planning Strategies for World Evangelization.* Grand Rapids: Eerdmans, 1980.

Dowley, Tim, John H. Y. Briggs, Robert D. Linder, and David F. Wright, eds. *Eerdmans' Handbook to the History of Christianity.* Grand Rapids: Eerdmans, 1977.

Grudem, Wayne. *Systematic Theology, An Introduction to Biblical Doctrine.* Grand Rapids: Zondervan, 1994.

Gundry, Patricia. *Woman Be Free!* Grand Rapids: Zondervan, 1977.

Hamon, Bill. *Prophets and the Prophetic Movement.* Shippensburg, Pa.: Destiny Image, 1990.

Harrison, Everet F. *The Apostolic Church.* Grand Rapids: Eerdmans, 1985.

Hatwin, George R. "The Ministry of the Apostle." *The Sharon Star* (April/May 1951).

Iverson, Dick, with Bill Scheidler. *Present Day Truths.* Portland, Oreg.: Bible Temple, 1975.

Jacobs, Cindy. *Possessing the Gates of the Enemy.* Grand Rapids: Chosen Books, 1991.

Kelly, J. N. D. *Early Christian Doctrines.* San Francisco: Harper-SanFrancisco, 1960.

Kroeger, Richard Clark, and Catherine Clark Kroeger. *I Suffer Not a Woman.* Grand Rapids: Baker, 1992.

Lea, Larry, with Judy Doyle. *Mending Broken Nets and Broken Fishermen.* Rockwall, Tex.: Church On The Rock, 1985.

McBirnie, William Steuart. *The Search for the Twelve Apostles.* Wheaton, Ill.: Tyndale House, 1978.

———. *The Search for the Early Church.* Wheaton, Ill.: Tyndale House, 1978.

Ministries Manual. Summerville, S.C.: Resurrection Churches and Ministries, 1992.

Murphy, Ed. *Spiritual Gifts and the Great Commission.* Pasadena: William Carey Library, 1975.

Scheidler, Bill. *The New Testament Church and Its Ministries.* Portland, Oreg.: Bible Temple, 1980.

Seton, Bernard E. "Should Our Church Ordain Women? No." *Ministry* (March 1985): 16, 17.

Shapiro, Joseph P., Joannie M. Schrof, Mike Tharp, and Dorian Friedman. "Honor Thy Children." *U.S. News and World Report* (February 27, 1995): 39.

Shibley, David. *A Force in the Earth.* Altamonte Springs, Fla.: Creation House, 1989.

Synan, Vinson. "Who Are the Modern Apostles?" *Ministries Today* (March/April 1992).

Tan, Paul Lee. *Encyclopedia of 7,700 Illustrations: Signs of the Times.* Rockville, Md.: Assurance Publishers, 1979.

The Amplified Bible. Grand Rapids: Zondervan, 1964.

Trombley, Charles. *Who Said Women Can't Teach?* South Plainfield, N.J.: Bridge Publishing, 1985.

Truscott, Graham. *What Does the Bible Teach About Women's Ministry?* Calgary, Alberta: Gordon Donaldson Missionary Foundation, 1979.

Vine, W. E. *An Expository Dictionary of New Testament Words.* Grand Rapids: Revell, 1966.

Wagner, C. Peter, "New Equipment for the Final Thrust," *Ministries Today* (January/February 1994).

————. *Your Spiritual Gifts Can Help Your Church Grow.* Ventura, Calif.: Regal, 1979; revised edition, 1994.

Williams, Don. *The Apostle Paul and the Women in the Church.* Van Nuys, Calif.: Bim Publishing, 1977.

Winter, Ralph D., and Steven C. Hawthorne, eds. *Perspectives on the World Christian Movement.* Pasadena: William Carey Library, 1992.

Witherington, Ben, III. *Women and the Genesis of Christianity.* Cambridge: Cambridge University Press, 1990.

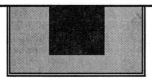

INDEX

Learn to Fight on Your Knees.

There's a battle raging, an unseen struggle in the heavens that affects the way we live as Christians. But how can you fight against a force which can't be seen, an invisible enemy desperate to foil God's plan? The answer is prayer. That's because the battle against Satan has already been won, paid for by the price of Christ's blood. You can discover the truth behind spiritual warfare and what you can do to advance the cause of Christ around the world through these factual, biblical guides from Regal Books.

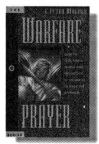 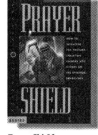 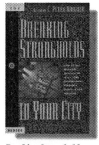 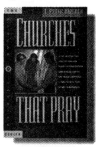